The Truth Will Set You Free

THE TRUTH WILL SET YOU FREE

Samuel L. Hoard

CONCORDIA PUBLISHING HOUSE · SAINT LOUIS

Unless otherwise indicated, all Scripture quotations are taken from the HOLY BIBLE, NEW INTERNATIONAL VERSION®. NIV®. Copyright © 1973, 1978, 1984 by International Bible Society. Used by permission of Zondervan Publishing House. All rights reserved.

Scripture quotations marked KJV are from the King James or Authorized Version of the Bible.

Quotations from Martin Luther's Small Catechism taken from *Luther's Small Catechism with Explanation* (St. Louis: Concordia, 1986, 1991).

Permission to reprint "From the Front Line" (p. 111) granted by *Lutheran Forum*.

Permission to print as a composite cover illustration © Flip Schulke/CORBIS and © The Miami Herald/David Walters.

Library of Congress Cataloging-in-Publication Data

Hoard, Samuel L.
   The truth will set you free / Samuel L. Hoard.
      p. cm.
   ISBN 0-7586-0547-1
   1. Hoard, Samuel L. 2. Lutheran Church—Missouri Synod—Clergy—Biography.
   3. African American clergy—Biography. I. Title.
   BX8080.H53A3 2004
   284.1'092—dc22   2004007461

2   3   4   5   6   7   8   9   10   13   12   11   10   09   08   07   06   05   04

CONTENTS

If you hold to My teaching,
you are really My disciples.
Then you will know the truth,
and the truth will set you free.

(John 8:31–32)

INTRODUCTION

Someone has said that we should forget the past and concentrate on moving forward. However, this would mean foregoing valuable lessons from that past—lessons we need if we are to live competently in the future.

I am black. I cannot forget my past and the encounters with racism that I have had in the church and in society. Both black and white people can profit from a backward look. There are lessons to be learned that can help us avoid the mistakes of the past and that can encourage us to persevere as we move into the future.

Racism is the conviction that solely because of race one group of people is superior to another. The actions and words of racist people will inevitably penalize, restrict, or cause pain to those of another race. Not all expressions and acts of racism are vicious or overt. However, unintentional acts can be as painful as deliberate ones. None of these acts should be tolerated in a free society, much less in the church of Jesus Christ.

But I relate my experiences with hope: that some black youth may be encouraged to "drive on" despite racist obstacles; that some of my fence-sitting white friends will have their eyes opened; that seeing they will believe, and believing they will act to expose and eliminate the racism around them. Finally, I hope to open the eyes of some of my black colleagues in the ministry who have wondered aloud, "Doesn't Sam know he's black?" Some of these friends have mistakenly concluded that a black student who attends white schools has been deprived of the "black experience." I believe that my experiences contradict that assumption.

I have lived and worked primarily within the Lutheran Church, attending schools in Fort Wayne, Indiana, and St. Louis, Missouri. The experiences I have had with racism in these institutions are not unique. The names of other predominantly white church bodies, schools, cities, or communities could be substituted. The prevailing attitudes toward black people were much the same in various institutions and regions of the United States when I was growing up.

From time to time I am asked why I remained in the Lutheran Church when racism was so prevalent. My response always has been to assume the stance of a child who suddenly learns that a parent has been struck with some terrible disease. A loving child does not throw up his arms in disgust and desert his mother or father. He stays by his parent's side and does everything possible to get rid of the affliction. I love the Lutheran Church and the simple Gospel of Christ that is proclaimed in this church body. It is my resolve to stand by her as a loyal son and to do all that I can to remove the blight of racism.

1

GROWING UP
IN ST. LOUIS

S t. Louis, Missouri, a city that sided with the North during the Civil War, never had segregation laws on its books, with the exception of its school system. Racial discrimination, however, was a real and active part of everyday life in St. Louis, as it was in New York City; Birmingham, Alabama; and every other part of the United States. Throughout our childhood, my friends and I were always aware of the influence of racism in our lives.

In the early 1920s, my parents traveled from Mississippi to Missouri and settled in St. Louis to raise our family of three girls and two boys. My father had been given the name Robert Lee Hoard. Although he had never considered any Southern general to be his hero, he named my older brother Robert Lee Hoard Jr., ignoring the irony of giving a black child such an inappropriate name.

During the 1920s, my father was a Pullman porter on the railroad. It was a good job for an unskilled black man in those days. When there was a split among the workers over the question of whether to organize the Brotherhood of Sleeping Car Porters as a union, my father supported the group in favor of the union. They were successful in organizing the union (the first black-organized union in the United States) under the leadership of A. Philip Randolph, but some men lost their jobs as a result, including my father. Because of his support, however, my father was made an honorary member of the Brotherhood of Sleeping Car Porters for life. Later he was employed at the main post office in St. Louis. My father retired from his position with the post office a few years before his death in 1959.

My mother had to work to supplement the family income. Three or four days a week she would rise early in the morning and ride several streetcars to the St. Louis suburbs of Clayton and Ladue to work as a laundress and housekeeper for wealthy white families. I can still remember how glad we were when my mother would bring home what people used to call "Thank-you-Ma'am bags." These contained things that were being discarded by "Mister Charlie" or "Miss Ann"—faded, frayed, and worn sport shirts; toys that were broken beyond repair; or even a turkey or pheasant carcass with a few slivers of meat that was left over from a banquet held the night before.

My mother's first name, Leah, came from the Bible, and her good, Southern, middle name was Belle. Tall, dark brown, and stately, my mother looked to me like an African princess. She lived with her well-worn Bible and practiced her Christian beliefs 24 hours a day. In piety and the practice of Christian virtues, she set a good example for her children. I was still quite young when she taught me a saying attributed to Booker T. Washington: "Never let any man pull you so low as to make you hate him." I took that to heart. While I have pity for and sometimes anger against those who are racist, I cannot hate them.

My mother sacrificed much and did all that she could for my sisters, my brother, and me as we were growing up. She had courage, determination, and physical stamina to spare. I saw in her the fruit of the Spirit described by St. Paul in Galatians 5. She died in 1992, only a month before her 102nd birthday. Serving God by serving others, she worked even in her 80s on behalf of the spiritual interest of boys and girls through the Christian Release Time Education Program of the city of Los Angeles. The most fitting description of her comes from the words of St. Mark (14:8a): "She did what she could."

School Days

During my elementary school years, I attended Sunday school at my mother's Pentecostal church. My neighbor and good friend Ray Finley and his family were members of the local Lutheran church. When I was in second grade, I was allowed to bring Ray with me to Sunday school and the following Sunday I attended Sunday school with him. I clearly remember that experience. At Ray's Sunday school, I heard positive and comforting messages about a Jesus who loves children, who loves and forgives sinners, who came to save sinners from that place called hell. Even as a second-grader, I knew all about hell. At my Sunday school it seemed that all we heard were terrible warnings against smoking, dancing, playing cards, reading comic strips, and playing marbles. I was convinced that hell would be bursting at the seams because a person did not have much of a chance to stay out.

After our exchange, I felt that the Lutheran Sunday school would be the one for me. I was given permission to attend Ray's Sunday school, and in the mid-1930s, through the influence of the Finley family, I became a member of St. Philip Lutheran

Church. Our pastor, Rev. Dr. Andrew Schulze, was a strong influence in my life and in the lives of many of the young members of St. Philip. An evangelical yet forceful man, Rev. Schulze worked for love and justice in the church and in society. During his active ministry, Rev. Schulze was frequently the object of scorn, but in a Christlike way, he insisted that Christians must work for racial inclusiveness, especially in the church. Rev. Schulze always impressed me as one of the most saintly and evangelical pastors in The Lutheran Church—Missouri Synod.

My interest in the Lutheran ministry began early and continued through my high school years. It was strengthened by the gentle question that Rev. Schulze would put to the young boys in the congregation: "Did you ever think about becoming a pastor?" I cannot point to a particular dramatic moment when I heard the voice of God say, "Samuel, Samuel, I want you to serve Me!" But I think Rev. Schulze planted the seed; God's Spirit did the rest.

Racism in St. Louis

My friends and I learned the lessons of racism early in our lives. Occasionally we would ride our bicycles north to O'Fallon Park or west toward Forest Park. The hot summer sun would make any normal boy thirsty. We knew, however, that our business was not wanted at the refreshment stands along our route. If we tried to buy a soft drink, we might have it shoved at us discourteously, if we were served at all. We could not even buy a glass of water. Our lot was to suffer, to grin and bear it, until we could return to the "Ville," as our section of St. Louis was called.

Fairgrounds Park was another forbidden place. More than once we heard the warning: "Although it is a public park, the white people who live nearby do not like our people, so the best thing is to stay away." My older brother, Rob, seemed to enjoy repeatedly learning the lessons of racism firsthand. Despite the warnings, Rob, who was probably 13 or 14 years old, had to find out about Fairgrounds Park for himself. One day he decided to try crawfishing in the lake at the Park, and he took me with him. (I was probably about 10 years old.) Whether the crawfish were biting that day or not, we will never know. We had scarcely dropped our lines in the water when a dozen or so large boys came running toward us, wielding snake skins and belts and yelling curses and threats. "Niggers! Niggers! Get them!" they cried. We had dared to breach the sanctity of "their" public park. Two very frightened black brothers forgot about crawfish. We ran as though our lives depended on it, and I believe they did. I do not know how many other black youth became good at track, but I began my training that day at Fairgrounds Park while running for my life. I have been an ace sprinter ever since.

The effects of racism in the St. Louis public schools was felt by all young people, white and black. In the 1930s, the entire St. Louis public school system was racially segregated. The white students were being miseducated about their superiority; the black students were being miseducated about their inferiority. However, in some respects, we felt that the system worked to our advantage. For example, Otis E. Finley Jr., my friend Ray's father, was the football and track coach at one of the two high schools for black students. He was a tall rather handsome man who stressed both the fundamentals and the fine points of football to his players. He worked conscientiously, eating, drinking, sleeping, studying, and talking football in season and out. Because of the segregation policy in the school system, black students had the opportunity to play football under one of the best coaches in the city.

Racial segregation in the St. Louis schools was so rigidly enforced that students attending black high schools were not allowed to compete in athletic events against students of white schools. The black high school teams had to travel to places such as Kansas City, Missouri; Louisville, Kentucky; Evansville, Indiana; and Memphis, Tennessee, to find similarly segregated competition. This was an example of the expense to all taxpayers when the doctrine of racism was allowed to prevail. But we loved those trips! What other high school team in St. Louis could boast of a schedule that included several hundred miles of road trips?

My World War II Experience

Before I even graduated from high school, I served a short stretch in the U.S. Marine Corps in 1945, near the end of World War II. But my enlistment was unexpectedly affected by a fractured leg I sustained during football practice. When I was taken to St. Louis City Hospital, my injury was treated by a medical intern who was dressed in a tweed suit rather than in hospital scrubs. Apparently he had been more concerned about not getting any plaster of paris on his suit than forming the cast properly over my fractured fibula. Consequently, when a teaching doctor later brought a group of interns to examine me, it was pointed out that the cast on my leg had been improperly applied. The doctor moved on to the next case, leaving behind no instructions for corrective action to be taken. The cast remained on my leg, even past the original date the hospital's clinic had scheduled to have it removed. After consulting with our family doctor, who was in his 80s, I removed the cast myself and began to walk on the leg without the aid of a crutch or a cane. This turned out to be a premature return to full use of the leg.

In April 1945, I turned 18. As required by law, I notified my draft board that I would be re-enrolled in high school the following September with only one half year to complete before graduation. I requested to be deferred from the draft to finish high school. However, I was notified that I would be drafted. Therefore, I decided to enlist early so I could complete basic training during the summer.

My choice of branches was the Marines because the ban on allowing black citizens to serve in the U.S. Marine Corps had recently been abolished. We had heard from news reports that one of the first black Marines had proudly gone on leave in his dress blues only to be arrested by some well-meaning but ignorant Southern law enforcement officers for "impersonating" a Marine. To get into the Marines in those days, you had to sit with those who had selected the Navy and hope and pray that the Marine sergeant would choose you when he came to pick his quota of personnel. My prayers were answered. I was one of five St. Louis draftees at that time who was chosen to become a Marine.

When we arrived at Camp Lejeune, North Carolina, for boot camp, I was shocked to see that it was racially segregated. I was even more shocked at the gutter language used by those in charge of the training. The cursing and abuse of God's name disturbed me so much that I mentioned it when I wrote home to my pastor, but I had forgotten about Rev. Schulze's practice of including in the Sunday bulletin small quotes from the letters he received from men in uniform. (Some letters were from fellows a little older than I who had become Tuskegee Airmen, including John Squires, who was killed in a crash in Italy, Otis Finley, and William Wyatt). Later, I was embarrassed to learn that Rev. Schulze reported: "Sam Hoard writes that he is surprised and disturbed about the offensive and sinful language he finds where he is stationed for basic training in the Marine Corps." People who saw this were no doubt saying, "What did Sam expect to find in the military? How naïve can he be?"

My career in the Marine Corps during World War II was short-lived. I discovered that my fractured leg had "drawn up," or shortened, when it healed. In addition, I had been born with a congenital condition in which my hip on the same side as my fractured leg was lower than the other side. I should have been wearing a lift in the heel of the shoe of my shortened leg to restore proper balance. Couple this with the fact that everywhere a "boot" goes during training is at double-time, that is, running, and I was going from sick bay to duty to sick bay to duty. In less than four months, my career in the Marine Corps was aborted. First came the announcement of the war's end, followed almost immediately by my discharge orders because of my leg. I may not have helped end the war in Asia or Europe, but my short enlistment made me eligible for the GI Bill—something that would come in handy later.

During those few months in the Marine Corps, far from home, I did some serious thinking and praying about my future. Was God calling me to become a pastor? By the time I graduated from high school, I felt certain that God wanted me in the ministry.

2

FINDING A PLACE TO BEGIN

There were three seminaries that offered training for the ministry in The Lutheran Church—Missouri Synod. The first was Immanuel Lutheran College and Seminary, a segregated school in Greensboro, North Carolina. As with nearly all "separate but equal" institutions and facilities, this seminary was separate but not equal. Had I enrolled there, I would have been the third student in the entire seminary department for 1946. Plus the school was located in the South. I had grown up with stories of the physical brutality and humiliation endured by black people who lived below the Mason-Dixon line. I admired the students for their courage in living with overt racism, but I decided against studying in Greensboro.

The second possibility was Concordia Seminary, St. Louis. I believed that this school was not a realistic choice for me because of its language requirements. Students were required to have completed a two-year program in Latin, German, and Greek at one of the church's preparatory colleges before entering the seminary. While at the seminary, students had to complete a course in Hebrew. I felt that I would not be able to meet these requirements because I was not a linguist. In high school I had studied with some of the best Latin teachers but had been among the worst students in class.

I felt strongly that a full-time vocation as a Christian pastor was what God wanted for me, and it was certainly what I wanted, so I turned to the third possibility. Concordia Theological Seminary in Springfield, Illinois, was for men who had made the decision to serve God in the holy ministry later in life. At the time, a college degree was not required for admission, and the language requirements were not as strict. So I applied. But in 1946, I and several other black applicants were turned down for admission.

Rev. Schulze, an alumnus of Concordia Theological Seminary, learned the reason: Racism in the church had triumphed again. Of course, the defenders of the status quo were not bold enough to tell me or the other applicants the truth. Instead, the letter of rejection enthusiastically encouraged me to enroll at the seminary in Greensboro. The irony was that at the turn of the 20th century, several decades before my rejection, black students had matriculated at the Springfield seminary.

My family members and friends wondered what my response would be to such a rejection. The obvious choice would have been to enroll in the segregated school in North Carolina. Or I could "throw in the towel" and let the ranks of the Lutheran ministry be filled by those with the "right" skin color and those few brave black men who had attended the Greensboro seminary. Neither of these choices was acceptable to me. I was determined to enter the Lutheran ministry and become a Lutheran pastor. Another rebuff caused by racism was not going to turn me from this goal.

Applying to Prep School

There was only one thing to do. In the spring of 1946, I sent letters of application to three of the church's preparatory colleges that offered the courses that were prerequisite for admission to the seminary in St. Louis. This meant that I would spend at least two years in the preparatory college, three years at the seminary, and one year as an intern in a parish before my graduation from the seminary. My goal of being ordained was at least six years away—several years more than would have been required had I been accepted at the Springfield seminary. When I thought about this "wasted time," I was almost ready to remain a layman. Encouragement from my mother helped me to remain patient and determined.

The answers to my letters of application did not arrive immediately, and I had time to think about the coming months and years of my education. I was concerned about the prospect of being the first or only black student enrolled at the school. My background in languages was poor. I thought I would flunk out and be an embarrassment to Rev. Schulze. But Rev. Schulze gave me some good advice: "Sam," he said, "you must remember that when you go to school they will not expect you to know all the subject matter before you arrive. You are going there for the purpose of learning." Rev. Schulze's oldest son, Paul, was already attending the St. Louis seminary, and he had told me about the requirements and procedures for enrollment. Also during the summer of 1946, he tutored me in Latin and introduced me to Greek.

Students from Concordia Seminary often visited St. Philip Lutheran Church to sing in the choir or to work with the Sunday school or the young people. One of these students was Jeff Johnson, who had attended The Lutheran Church—Missouri Synod preparatory college in Oakland, California. In 1946 he was vice president of the student body at the St. Louis seminary, but most important, he was black like me—maybe a little more handsome but black nevertheless. He was making the grade. Why shouldn't I?

During that long waiting period, family and friends supplied encouragement and one additional thing: prayer. Prayer relieved my fears and gave me the needed self-confidence. Finally I received a letter in response to my application to Concordia Junior College in Fort Wayne, Indiana. I was accepted! Not until several years later did I learn why the response had taken so long. When my application was received in late summer 1946, the members of the Board of Control of Concordia Junior College had to meet to consider the application of a potential student who was a black Lutheran, evidently the first such application to be received by the college.

Because of the illness of the president, Rev. Dr. Elmer Foelber was serving as acting president. A professor of English and humanities, Dr. Foelber was a good teacher as well as an excellent musician. He also was a man of integrity and sincere Christian faith. Many times I have expressed gratitude to God that Dr. Foelber was acting president when my application to Concordia Junior College was being considered.

It was reported later that during the decision-making process, one board member cautioned the others that one could not be too sure about Negroes. He remembered from his childhood that the Negroes used to steal the chickens from his father's farm in Missouri. During the meeting, the president reportedly sent word from his sickbed that if a black student were accepted for the first time on this small campus, he probably would suffer a recurrence of his illness. Another member of the board was reported to have warned against making an affirmative decision in this matter. He pointed out that the four-year high school, which was operated on the same campus as the college, was co-educational. Thus white girls were present on campus. In response to this warning, Acting President Foelber asked, "If we do accept this black student, just what do you think our girls are going to do to him?" Dr. Foelber was then accused of being a "Negro lover," but he quickly pointed out the logical assumption that the name-caller must be a "Negro hater."

Of course there were some genuine and color-blind Christians on that board of Concordia Junior College, and Dr. Foelber was one of them. To these people, skin color made no difference. I am confident that the fears of the overly cautious members of the board were eventually assuaged. During my stay on the Fort Wayne campus, I did not marry nor date a white girl, nor was I caught or held on suspicion of stealing a single chicken. On the other hand, twice I won and once I was runner-up as the most-popular male college student in the Student Popularity Contest conducted jointly with the high school and college departments.

When my application was received in 1946, however, there was real consternation. The letter I received in response to my application was indicative of the extent to which racism was active in the Lutheran Church. In part the letter said (1) I could not be accepted as a dormitory student because it was rather late when my application was received and the dormitories were all filled. (2) The boys enrolled at the junior college were not accustomed to living in close quarters with Negroes. (3) It was possible that I could be accepted as a day student, but this was doubtful because there were no Negro Lutherans in Fort Wayne at that time and I would be unable to find a place to board in town. (4) The board members had learned that my application had been turned down at the Springfield seminary and that the officials there had strongly urged me to make application at The Lutheran Church—Missouri Synod seminary for Negroes at Greensboro, North Carolina. While the letter did not reject my application, the obstacles to my actual attendance at Concordia Junior College were clearly stated.

In the 1940s, most of the Lutheran churches in Fort Wayne had formed a missionary association. The association had extended a call to Rev. Paul G. Amt to serve as a so-called "Negro missionary." There were no black Lutherans in this city where Lutherans, for more than one hundred years, had been establishing congregations and preaching the universal Gospel of Jesus Christ. Pastor Amt accepted the call, leaving a successful pastorate in Philadelphia, where his congregation was predominantly black. He knew the problems, the hopes, and the goals of black people, as well as the continuing problem of racism within and outside the church. Pastor Amt was white but well-qualified for this new assignment. His primary task would be to win converts for the Lutheran Church among the black citizens of Fort Wayne.

Pastor Amt learned of my predicament and the slim chance I had of being allowed to enroll at Concordia Junior College. He arranged for my room and board in the lovely home of the elderly wife of a black doctor. The doctor himself had been confined to a nursing home following a stroke. Thus I was accepted as a day student at Concordia and finally was ready to begin my training for the ministry.

3

GETTING STARTED

The Concordia Junior College Board of Control must have thought that to allow a black student to enroll as a day student was one thing but to permit one to live in a dormitory was another. In all schools, it is not long after the start of the school year before a few students find it necessary to drop out. Thus dormitories suddenly have space available. I assumed that because I had been accepted as a bona fide student I would be able to move into the dorm without any problem as soon as there was a vacancy.

I found such a vacancy in a four-man room. After one student left campus, the remaining occupants were two pre-ministerial high school students, Jules Bush from Cleveland and Milton Kionka from Detroit, and one college student, Louie Dorn, from Cleveland. I spoke to Louie about the possibility of moving into the room, and he assured me that he would not mind. He did feel, however, that he should check with the other two students. When they agreed, I thought I was in. Much to my chagrin, I discovered that I would have to await the approval of the members of the Board of Control. Because I was the first black student admitted to Concordia, the board would have to discuss the matter at its monthly meeting.

The house where I was staying on Eliza Street was close to the campus and was more than satisfactory, but for a student away from home, it could not take the place of dormitory living. Much learning goes on in dormitories aside from the mutual aid one can provide and receive in preparing lessons for the classroom. I needed all the help I could get, especially in the Latin, German, and Greek courses to which I had been assigned. I needed help with translation, declension, and even pronunciation of all those languages. I could not receive this help sitting alone in my room on Eliza Street. Sometimes I wished for the Holy Spirit's gift of tongues about which the members of my mother's Pentecostal church often boasted! I felt that not to be permitted to move into that dormitory would mean the sudden end of any chance I might have to make a passing grade in languages and possibly other courses as well.

While I was waiting for a vacancy in the dorms, I became acquainted with Bob Epp, an upperclassman who was in charge of the high school students in his suite. Bob and I had something in common that the other students did not have: Both of us had served in the Marines. While stationed in Japan, Bob had become involved in the outstanding work being done at an orphanage by a group of Lutheran deaconesses. He wanted to return there, perhaps as a teacher.

In his capacity as proctor, Bob was an unusually strict disciplinarian and careful to enforce the rules. Occasionally I would stay on campus for the evening chapel service and remain to make preparations for the next day's quiz in Latin, German, or

Greek. Bob not only would invite me to use his study room but also to spend the night on the couch when I stayed on campus. Someone informed the president of this, and, ironically for Bob, we were both cited for an infraction of the rules. No one was allowed to remain overnight in the dorm without the president's special authorization.

I might still be waiting for the Concordia Junior College Board of Control to consider my simple request to live in the dorm had it not been for Pastor Amt. The board met in October and again in November 1946 with the same results: There was too much other business on the agenda to consider my request. I told Pastor Amt emphatically that if the board could not put my request on the agenda and give me an affirmative answer by the time I was ready to leave for Christmas vacation, I would not return to the campus. I planned to apply to Concordia in Oakland, California, where Jeff Johnson had successfully matriculated without the racism that I was being forced to endure.

Because of the special work he was called to do in Fort Wayne, Pastor Amt was as eager as I for the board's decision. He spoke with some of the board members, telling them that I would not return if the decision about my living arrangements was not made soon and in the affirmative. I imagine that the response from some of these people was "Good!" However, Pastor Amt also let it be known that if I did not return after Christmas as a bona fide dormitory student, he and his family would leave Fort Wayne. He pointed out that he could not effectively serve as their so-called "Negro missionary" if, on the one hand, he was being told by Lutheran congregations to win converts and, on the other hand, people from these same congregations refused to treat fairly the only black Lutheran who was already in their midst.

Pastor Amt and his entire household—his wife, his four children, and his mother-in-law—provided encouragement and waited anxiously with me for the board's approval of my move into the dormitory. Everyone was elated when Pastor Amt conveyed to me the news that the board had finally decided to take a bold, brash, and precedent-setting step: The first black student at Concordia Junior College could move into the dormitory when school resumed after Christmas vacation.

Racism at College

I left Fort Wayne for my first Christmas vacation in December 1946. After the long frustrating days of waiting for a decision on my request to move into the dorm, I was glad to be going home. My relatives and friends, however, insisted on giving me more advice and counsel than I wanted to hear. I was told that I carried a tremendous responsibility on my shoulders; that I was paving the way for others of my race; that I had to study hard and not spoil the chances for others to be accepted at that school. I wanted very much to tell these people that I was only a man attending school to learn like any other student. I did not think of myself as a trailblazer. I was having enough trouble making the grade on my own without worrying about bearing the burden of all black Lutheran young people on my shoulders. I wanted to tell everyone to give some advice to the Board of Control of Concordia Junior College, not to me! But I bit my tongue and forced a smile to keep from arguing.

My mother already had admonished me on the subject of my association with white girls. I was well aware that this was a serious concern for a black student at a white school, and I also knew that friendship between white and black males was apt to suffer severe strain if the black male even suggested the possibility of a date with a white female. Many of the white female students I met were far less bigoted than their male counterparts, but I had imposed dating restrictions on myself to avoid any kind of misunderstanding. While I had no prejudice against people who were white, black, red, or yellow, I had no intention of jeopardizing my education by inviting racist harassment on this issue. I was determined that neither white girls nor racism nor curriculum nor anything else would sway me from my goal.

This determination was put to the test more than once. If I had known when I arrived in Fort Wayne that I would be attending that two-year college for four years, I am not sure I would have stayed. The first time I saw my schedule of classes, I seriously thought of taking the next train back to St. Louis. I began my first year with special accelerated classes in German and Greek, in addition to classes in Latin and the other required courses. More than once I had to remind myself of Rev. Schulze's advice: "Sam, you are going there to learn."

My college classmates came from Lutheran elementary and high schools or from northern middle-class white school systems. I came from the segregated school system in St. Louis, which was scholastically below the national average, and even this education had been interrupted. Those classmates who had attended parochial high schools had followed an intensive program of language study: four years of Latin, three years of German, and two years of Greek. Those classmates who had attended public schools usually were allowed to complete their preparatory training in three years. It was decided by the dean that my training would be extended over a four-year period.

I did not need any reminders from my family or friends that I was the first and only black student on the Concordia campus. I was very aware of the unmistakable signs of racism, though most of what I saw and heard was the result of ignorance and insensitivity rather than a conscious intention to express racial animosity. Shortly after I arrived, I noticed that there were two college freshmen who spoke in an Amos 'n' Andy dialect every time I was within hearing distance. Anyone should be able to endure a little good-natured teasing, but this became a constant irritation. One of my classmates, realizing that I was becoming infuriated, asked what was troubling me. I explained to him that I did not understand the significance of this dialect. If the two students were trying to make me feel at home, their efforts were in vain because my family and friends in St. Louis did not speak that way. The message got back to the two students, Martin Behrens and Warren Priehs, and soon they came to me with profuse apologies. We became good friends.

I recall a particularly bitter experience when one classmate in a group I was with issued an invitation for a weekend visit to his home. Thinking that I was included, I started to reply that it sounded like a great idea but I had to stay on campus and study. Before I could finish my sentence, I was interrupted with the crushing, unexpected rebuff: "I wasn't including you; I'm not taking any 'zigaboo' home with me!"

There were numerous incidents when classmates, professors, and others in ordinary conversation, in everyday language, in behavior, demonstrated the extent to which their thinking had been stained by racism. I remember the religion class that broke out in peals of laughter the day I was called on to recite a passage from Psalm 51: "Purge me with hyssop, and I shall be clean; wash me, and I shall be whiter than snow" (KJV). The laughter was not cruel; the students were embarrassed and painfully self-conscious about race.

One of my professors had the habit of using the expression "There must have been a nigger in the woodpile somewhere" to indicate that there was a problem. There was no indication that he was going to stop using this phrase after I appeared in his classroom. In my conversations with this professor concerning classwork, I made it a point never to broach the subject of woodpiles, their sizes, the possibilities of people hiding in them, nor the many plausible reasons one might have for hiding in them. It is true that long-held habits are difficult to change, and perhaps he did not even realize what he was saying, but it did seem to me that out of a sense of decency he might have refrained from talking about "niggers" in the presence of a black student who not only was not in the woodpile but also was right in front of him in his classroom.

Shortly after I was elected president of the male chorus, the director asked us to rehearse the song "Kentucky Babe." Some of the words are "Sleep, Kentucky Babe, . . . Lay your kinky, woolly head on your Mammy's breast . . . Sleep, Kentucky Babe." These were not the days of growing pride in black identification, "black is beautiful," and wearing the hair natural by black youth. I was insulted and felt sick that I was asked to sing this song. Two of the students in the chorus volunteered to speak to the director for me. I simply wanted him to understand exactly how I felt about this particularly offensive selection. The director's response was that he could see nothing in the lyrics of the song that could be offensive to me. Therefore, the chorus would continue to rehearse that piece of music. They did; my two friends and I did not.

I have often thought how difficult life must be when black persons who pass for white and are considered part of the majority group must listen to racial slurs made in their presence. I think most of the racist slips made in my presence have been inadvertent and the result of thoughtlessness. But they have been insulting nonetheless. I was invited to have Sunday dinner with a family in Fort Wayne. During the conversation at the table, one son spoke enthusiastically about his summer job of mowing lawns for the public parks department. He talked about how much he liked the job, and one of the big advantages was the chance to get a good suntan without much effort. He explained that it would not take too many days before he was "almost as black as a nigger."

There was another slip-of-the-tongue incident that seemed to suggest I had been accepted into the group of my classmates. I had acquired a 1929 Dodge and, with some of my classmates, was driving back to the campus after playing an exciting, exhausting game of baseball. We were physically tired but spirited; there was a feeling of careless camaraderie. One of the riders noticed a brand-new convertible coming toward us and called out, "Look at that car! Isn't that a fine..." Before he finished the sentence, the car was close enough for us to see the occupants. The acclamations turned to sneers, and the student said, "Look at that—niggers in it. Isn't that a shame!"

No one said a word. I was shocked, then disgusted, that no one else spoke up to give him a lecture. I wondered if everyone in my car felt the same way. Then I realized that the person who had made the racial slip was painfully embarrassed. I had to conclude that he felt "at home" with me and had accepted me completely as another student with the same interests and purpose in life as his own. Race relations are complicated!

Christian Acceptance

Looking back on those four years in Fort Wayne, I must admit that the memories of pleasant experiences far outweigh the recollections of the difficult times when I felt the sting of racism. I found that there were professors, students, and even members of the Board of Control who had a deep Christian concern for people as individual human beings no matter what color skin they had. My three roommates and Bob Epp were good friends to me. Darwood Kesselmayer invited me to spend a Christmas vacation at his home. Paul Erdman included me in an invitation to several students to spend a weekend at his home. Dr. Foelber consistently declared his stand against racism.

Another member of the Concordia Junior College board, Rev. Dr. Arno C. Scholz, was also pastor of Bethlehem Lutheran Church in Fort Wayne. One Sunday morning I was with a group of students who attended the Communion service at his church. I did what all serious-minded, faithful Lutherans are taught to do. I approached the altar and received the bread and wine. At this time nearly all Lutheran churches used the common cup for distribution of the wine to communicants. Two parishioners (a husband and wife) who also took Communion that morning apparently had never shared the same altar and the same cup with a black Christian. I was told later that this couple spoke to Rev. Scholz, saying that I had given offense to them. They threatened to join another congregation. Unable to reason with them, Rev. Scholz finally told them that there were six or seven other Lutheran churches to which he would gladly transfer their membership.

There were, I am sure, more than one couple like this in the Lutheran churches in Fort Wayne, but transferring membership was not really a solution to the problem. With some of my classmates, I visited different Lutheran churches from one Sunday to the next to hear different styles of preaching. Whenever the congregation celebrated Communion, I celebrated the Sacrament too.

Of course there were countless humorous stories about the absent-minded Professor Bente, one of our most respected professors. He taught English literature and was an authority on the teaching of logic, coaching some of the greatest debating teams in the Fort Wayne area. Harvard had tried to recruit him for its faculty, but his heart was in the work of helping to train future pastors for his church. He and his wife were not only gracious, but considering the era, they were bold to allow me to invite Betty

Gibson—a black Lutheran woman, fellow St. Louisan, and a student at Valparaiso University—to Fort Wayne as their houseguest over a homecoming weekend.

Another faculty member, Dr. John Stach, would often take a walk in the evening, sometimes strolling through that section of the city where many black families lived. He would say that he felt as safe walking through the black community as he did in any other area of Fort Wayne. This remark irritated some of his Lutheran friends, and occasionally he was called a "nigger lover." Dr. Stach's response was simple and direct: "Yes, as a Christian I do love these people, though I do not use the same despicable terminology that you use. I accept them as my brothers and sisters in Christ. I love them as my neighbors."

Concordia students were regularly welcomed to the homes of Lutheran families in the Fort Wayne area as Sunday dinner guests. This was known as the "Phils" system, which was derived from the Greek word *philos*, which means "friend." Shortly after I enrolled as a day student, Edgar Krentz, the second of three sons, asked me if I would like his family to become my "Phils." He told me that if I was interested he would check with his folks, but he was sure they would be happy to have me. I was not at all sure about that, and I wondered what the response would be when Ed announced, "Guess who's coming to dinner?" But Ed knew his family well, and they were indeed happy to have me as a regular Sunday visitor.

My association with the Krentz family brought me into contact with many Lutheran Christians who rejected any kind of racist behavior. As superintendent of the Lutheran Deaconess Association of The Lutheran Church—Missouri Synod, Pastor Krentz was often away from home, lecturing or preaching. When he was scheduled to speak in a church near Fort Wayne, he invited his Sunday guests (students from the college) to accompany him.

In this way I became acquainted with the Hugo Boerger and Erwin Fuelling families near Decatur, Indiana. They were farmers and well-off financially. The Boergers had three daughters; the Fuellings had only one son, and he wanted to become a farmer like his dad. Both men had hoped to have sons in the Lutheran ministry. Because this was not possible, they took pleasure in helping others who were preparing to be pastors. Our friendship lasted over the years, and I have never forgotten their generosity in giving me financial help when I desperately needed it.

The Krentz family had their membership at Redeemer Lutheran Church—an English District congregation with a strong liturgical tradition. I attended services with them occasionally. There I met the Kurth family. Rev. Dr. Erwin Kurth was Redeemer's pastor, an eloquent speaker, and one of the few pastors at that time who gave strong public support to the work being done by Pastor Amt. Pastor Kurth was not at all apprehensive about the racial integration of his congregation. I communed at the altar in his church on many memorable occasions. Pastor Kurth came to Fort Wayne from a parish in Brooklyn, New York. Many years later I accepted a call to become pastor of that same congregation, Our Savior's on Covert Street.

The Edwin Walda family lived across the street from the campus of Concordia Junior College, and many students came to know them as "Ma" and "Pa" Walda. I was as welcome in their spacious and friendly home as any other student. On my graduation day, I took my mother to the house to meet the Waldas. "Pa" was in the living room, talking with a business associate. After "Ma" opened the door and invited us into the house, she put her arms around me and gave me a big kiss, congratulating me on my graduation. My mother and I never forgot the look on the face of "Pa" Walda's business associate as he observed that color-blind display of affection.

In all these associations and experiences, I discovered that there were many white Lutheran Christians who not only rejected the prevailing doctrines of racism but also acted on those convictions in their daily lives.

4

LEARNING ABOUT THE CITY OF FORT WAYNE

There were some heartening occasions when members of the Concordia Junior College student body came to my aid in helping to confront and combat discrimination in public places in Fort Wayne. They helped not only me but also all members of my race and other minority people as well who, because of their skin color, were subject to discriminatory treatment or outright refusal of service in public places in Fort Wayne.

The first time I went with a classmate to a "greasy spoon" near Anthony Boulevard, we encountered racism, which was not new to me but was enlightening for my classmates. John Morton and I sat down at the counter. The man behind the counter took John's order for a hamburger but reacted to my presence as if I had committed some grievous personal offense against him. Finally, he scornfully inquired what I wanted to order, and I asked for a slice of lemon meringue pie. As if every effort pained him, the counterman placed the pie on a paper napkin and shoved it across the counter to me. I was willing to meet him halfway so he would not have to wash an extra dish, but I did request a fork. It was quite clear that he was not going to give me a fork. Calmly and politely I tried to explain that I intended to eat that pie right there, sitting next to my friend John, who was already devouring his hamburger. The counterman insisted that I had to take the pie outside to eat it. The suggestion might have been reasonable with a piece of cherry or apple pie, but who in his right mind would want to stand on a street corner, eating a piece of lemon meringue pie balanced on a paper napkin?

For a moment or two I tried to make it clear that I was determined to eat that piece of pie with a fork, sitting at the counter like any other Concordia student. Finally, I gave up. The counterman was in control of the supply of forks and was in a better position to get his point across. Disgusted by what was happening, John stopped eating in the middle of a bite, paid for his hamburger, and accompanied me back to the dormitory. We related the experience to another classmate, Dick Bolin, and he became so incensed that he wanted to return to the restaurant immediately. I tried to convince him that it would be useless, but he persuaded John and me to go with him to confront the counterman because of his discriminatory treatment of Concordia's black student.

When we tried to talk to the man, he was not only unfriendly but also evasive and uncooperative. He protested that he only worked at the restaurant; he was only carrying out orders; the discrimination was the manager's policy. When Dick asked for the manager's phone number, the man said he did not know what it was and only saw the manager once every three or four weeks.

Dick Bolin was a determined, serious-minded young man and did not intend to be put off by this man's lack of cooperation. He mapped out a strategy for us that he was sure would bring out the manager or the owner, and he recruited a number of students to help. They all went into the restaurant, gave their orders for hamburgers, French fries, hot dogs, milkshakes, pie a la modes, and so forth. At just the right moment—when the grill was loaded with hamburgers and hot dogs, when the French fries were almost finished, when the ice cream had been scooped on the slices of pie—I entered. Without exchanging greetings with any of the students, I ordered one piece of lemon meringue pie, which was shoved across the counter on a paper napkin with the expected instructions to eat it outside. Right on cue, the students spoke up: "If he can't eat the pie in here, I don't want my hamburger." "Cancel my French fries." "I don't want the pie a la mode." "Never mind the milkshake; I don't want it."

The frustrated, bewildered counterman phoned the manager, who arrived on the scene in record time. Dick and I talked with him, and finally he agreed that I would be served like any other Concordia student. I did, however, have to assure him that I would not race up and down Eliza, Hugh, and Lafayette Streets with a sign on my back and a megaphone in my hand, advertising to the black families in that area that if they came to the greasy spoon near Anthony Boulevard they would be allowed to eat their pie with forks!

Victory at the Soda Fountain

During 1947, my second year on campus, Dick Bolin and I were roommates. He worked downtown at the soda fountain of a drugstore that belonged to a nationwide chain. When I asked him about the store's policy on serving black people, he said he did not know, but he assured me that if I wanted to stop in, he would see to it that I was served. I did this twice, but before I had a chance to go a third time, the manager had been informed that Dick was transgressing one of the store's most sacred policies by serving a black customer. An angry Dick was willing to risk his job over this issue and begged me to return while he was working to request fountain service. I did go back, but not alone.

About this same time, the more active adults in the local branch of the NAACP were organizing a junior branch of the organization. Rev. Gilmartin, a Unitarian minister, and Mrs. Kinerk, a white woman, were among the adult advisors. The group included representatives from every high school in the city, as well as some college students. After one of our evening meetings, this interracial group went into this same drugstore, filling up the booths near the soda fountain. We seated ourselves so there were one or two black students in each booth. As expected, the waitresses told us they could serve only white people. In response, the white members of the group said, "We would like to be served, but we will not order unless you serve everyone."

Our entrance into the store coincided with the ending of the movies in the downtown theaters. The people from the movies were beginning to come in, waiting impatiently to be seated. The waitresses pleaded with us to leave. The white members of the group explained that they did want to be served but only when everyone was served. They were prepared to wait until closing time, if necessary. Joe Lyons, a young black friend, two adult advisors, and I were invited behind the prescription counter to consult with the manager. Blaming the officials of the drugstore chain for this policy of racial discrimination, the manager pleaded for more time to consult with these officials. We assured him that we could arrange for this interracial group of students to return to the store on Saturdays at noon and periodically at other times when the soda fountain was busy. Twenty-four hours later, the manager notified us, through Dick Bolin, that black and white people together would be served in that store without discrimination.

Other experiences I had with restaurateurs in Indiana convinced me that often discriminatory policies were not caused by bitter racial hatred but by a cool, calculated concern for cash. When our basketball team returned from a game in another city, we would be treated to a steak dinner in one of the restaurants near Fort Wayne. I was the only black person in this group of eighteen or twenty, and never to my knowledge was there any threat of refusal to serve all those steak dinners because one black youth was part of the group. On the other hand, if I went into one of those same restaurants with two or three white friends, a hush would fill the room. People would stop their conversations and stare as if something dreadful were about to happen. My friends and I would be greeted by the manager with, "I'm sorry; we cannot serve you here." I felt sorry for those people because I could detect embarrassment and a terrible fear of losing the dollars of their bigoted clientele.

During my years at Concordia Junior College, I did a lot of hitchhiking—to St. Louis, Los Angeles, Chicago, Detroit, and other places. Frequently I received rides from black truck drivers who had their own prejudices. They would tell me the only reason they stopped was because I was a "soul brother." When I expressed surprise and dismay that they would not stop for any of my white classmates, they would say, "No, sir. This rig won't stop for hitchhiking white folks. I don't trust any white folks. They're no good, not one of them." I learned from these conversations that if a person—white or black—is determined to keep a closed mind and be prejudiced, there is nothing much that can be done or said. I was never able to convince these drivers that they might be wrong.

Racism in the Church

Of all my experiences and associations in the city of Fort Wayne, none was more disappointing than my involvement with the mission efforts of Pastor Amt. I was able to help him to make contact with prospective black converts to Lutheranism. I made follow-up visits to people he had contacted, and I accompanied some of these people to Lutheran churches, explaining the order of worship and answering questions about the practices and customs of the Lutheran Church. In the long run, however, I was unable to help Pastor Amt stay in Fort Wayne and continue his work. The problem was too big and too deeply rooted for either of us to cope with successfully. No matter what delicate, cautious words were used to describe it, the problem was racism in the church.

There was at that time in Fort Wayne a comparatively small percentage of black people, and with the exception of one small area, their homes were scattered throughout the city. There was hardly one house in the city where a person standing on the front or back porch could not see the steeple of a Lutheran church. Many of the clergy and lay members of the missionary association in Fort Wayne expected their "Negro missionary" to carry out his work in the traditional way, establishing a separate-but-equal mission church for the "colored folk."

During his ministry, however, Pastor Amt had gained the confidence of more black people than the average white man, talking with the educated as well as the uneducated in the black community. He was able to get a frank opinion or a true expression of how black people felt about an integrated or a segregated approach to church work. Convinced that racial segregation was wrong, whether prompted by the false racial pride of black people or by the unwarranted feelings of superiority of white people, Pastor Amt refused to be hemmed in by a ministry that would keep him from declaring the complete, inclusive Gospel of Christ.

After making initial contacts, Pastor Amt would conduct a membership class, then confirm those who were ready to join the church. He would present or refer these new members to the established Lutheran churches nearest their homes.

Often in his work, Pastor Amt would make contact with white persons or persons from various minority groups who expressed an interest in the membership classes, and these people would be included too. It was soon apparent to the missionary association that Pastor Amt was doing his work in an unexpected way. Despite the rumblings against Pastor Amt's methods, some prominent laypersons and a few parish pastors publicly supported him, most notably Pastor Scholz, Pastor Kurth, and Pastor Fred Wambsganns. Others completely disapproved or vacillated about how they felt concerning these pioneering efforts. On the one hand, Pastor Amt had not established the "colored church" that had been envisioned. On the other hand, he was conducting interracial membership classes and expecting these people to be accepted and integrated into the existing Lutheran congregations.

The Board of Directors of the Fort Wayne Missionary Association did not approve of Pastor Amt's activities and strongly criticized the method he was using to win black converts for Christ. The board members felt that Pastor Amt was not doing what he had been called to do. Finally, Pastor Amt had to take a stand, and he demanded to know if he was expected to carry out his ministry according to traditional racist customs and only among black people, excluding any others who might seek to join The Lutheran Church—Missouri Synod. He pointed out that if the answer of the association was in the affirmative, then he could not, in good conscience, accept its call to him as being valid in the sight of God.

Not long after I graduated in 1950, Pastor Amt and his family left Fort Wayne. And not long after he left, a separate worship facility was set aside for black Lutherans. Many Lutheran Christians in Fort Wayne sacrificed time, energy, and effort to share the Gospel and themselves with others in the community, no matter their color. There were many, I am sure, who knew, deep in their hearts, that it was wrong to practice and encourage the idea that black Christians should deny and be denied fellowship with white Christians in the established churches in the city. Those who were responsible for this "separate but equal" facility must have felt some guilt for alienating the forward-thinking, self-respecting, progressive black Christians to whom encouragement of a segregated approach to worship, even in that day, was an affront to their dignity.

5

MY FIRST JOB
AS A SEAMAN

When the first fall 1949 issue of the *Maroon and White*, the Concordia Junior College paper, appeared, the headline of a feature article read: "Hoard Lands Job in New York as Seaman; Visits German Cities." The article began with my words: "As most of you know, jobs were at a premium this summer. Most college students had to wander around to land something worthwhile. I was in such a predicament this summer. . . . In fact, before I finally got a job I had to go all the way to New York City. But what a job it was!"

It was the summer before my fourth and final year at Concordia Junior College in Fort Wayne. A couple students and I had planned to stay the summer and find employment in Fort Wayne instead of returning to our hometowns. We were going to remain in a dormitory and do maintenance jobs around campus in lieu of rent, as a few students had been allowed to do the previous summer. However, those students had left the dormitories they were permitted to occupy in bad condition, which was not discovered until just before school was to resume. As a result, at the last minute we learned that no students would be allowed to remain in the dormitories over the summer.

What was I to do? To return home to St. Louis and seek the job I had held for the previous two summers was not possible. The St. Louis Board of Education was no longer hiring college students as playground recreational supervisors. How the idea surfaced to become a seaman for the summer I do not know. I didn't know how to seek employment aboard a ship. All I knew was that it would be pretty good pay, which I needed desperately at the time, and that ships traveled across the ocean to and from New York City. I was interested in traveling and was willing to do most any kind of work on any kind of ship—scrubbing decks, in the galley, as a waiter, anything that was available.

After bidding farewell to the other guys, I prepared for my trip to New York City. I would have to take the Pennsylvania Turnpike to get there. My ticket consisted of a large piece of cardboard with the words "TO PENN" written in black ink. Somehow I made it to the big city.

After safely arriving in New York City, the first thing I did was find the most inexpensive place to stay, which was a room at the Sloane House YMCA near midtown Manhattan. The second thing I did was locate Mount Zion Lutheran Church in Harlem (formerly St. Matthew's), an all-white congregation of The Lutheran Church—Missouri Synod that had relocated. Rev. Dr. Clemonce Sabourin, an African American, was the pastor there. Rev. Sabourin was instrumental, with the help of God's Spirit, in establishing one of the leading African American congregations and parochial schools in The Lutheran Church—Missouri Synod. I had met Rev. Sabourin when I was much younger because he was a close friend of my pastor, Rev. Schulze.

Rev. Sabourin was most encouraging and helpful. I needed a source of income until I could land my seaman's job. Besides being a good pastor and outstanding speaker and writer, Rev. Sabourin was an excellent carpenter. Mount Zion had a four-story building adjacent to the sanctuary. This building had housed not only a parochial school on the lower floors but also a comfortable parsonage and even a theater on the upper floors. That summer Rev. Sabourin was busy with some minor renovations in the school building. He graciously allowed me to earn subsistence money by doing menial tasks in the school building, such as washing the walls. This part-time work was convenient to my job-seeking schedule. When he and his wife on several occasions invited me to have dinner with them and their young son, I had the privilege of enjoying some of the most delicious meals. And "delicious" was not imagined because I was a nearly penniless student far from my mother's cooking. Mrs. Sabourin had a master's degree in home economics.

As it turned out, one of Rev. Sabourin's parishioners told me where to apply for a seaman's job. He said the procedure was to apply for a civil service job on a U.S. military sea transportation ship that shuttled military personnel, civilian dependents, and European displaced persons between Europe and the United States. The place to apply was at the shipyard in Brooklyn at 58th Street and First Avenue. To get a job, I had to do two things. First, I had to put down my experience in a needed occupation. Second, I had to obtain "seaman's papers."

While I was filling out the application, one of the African American seamen asked me if I had any experience "carrying a tray"—meaning as a waiter. I answered that I had been "carrying a tray" for the past three years. Of course, I was referring to carrying my tray through the cafeteria line in the dining hall at school.

For seaman's papers (a laminated card about the size of a driver's license), I had to apply at the U.S. Coast Guard station. This document listed what jobs I could do on board ship. A large room called the "Crewing Section" was located in this same building To receive an assignment to a ship, you had to report at the Crewing Section each morning by 8:30 A.M. Then a man would call out people's names and tell them to report to the Deck Department, the Engine Department, or the Steward Department. African Americans were never called to any section except the Steward Department, where they would be assigned to jobs such as cooks, waiters, and room stewards. Sometimes one or two whites would work as waiters, but it was strictly by choice rather than racial restriction or segregation. Black applicants were restricted or segregated into this department.

This reminded me of the case of Dorie Miller, a black American sailor. The U.S. Armed Forces were segregated in 1941 when the Japanese launched the surprise attack on Pearl Harbor. The Navy policy was that black Americans could be assigned only to the Steward Department. Although only assigned duty as a messman, in the heat of battle Miller manned one of the ship's anti-aircraft guns and shot down a couple Japanese planes. I could not keep from wondering why black people had to put up with this type of racism and when this illegal segregation in the military and government would really end.

After several more days of waiting, I became excited as I heard my name matter-of-factly called. Along with four other men, I was told to report to the Steward Department. Armed with my newly issued seaman's papers that endorsed me for employment in the Steward Department as utilityman/waiter, I was ready to become, for the first time, a seaman. Steward Department or not, I was elated to be hired.

The ship to which I was assigned as a crew member was the USS *General George W. Goethals.* I had confided to an experienced crew member that it had been some time since I had last been "carrying a tray." I admitted that I was a bit rusty on how to set a place properly. My confession soon found its way to the second steward who was directly in charge of assigning waiters to particular stations. I was assigned to wait on tables reserved for the ship's officers. It meant earning less in tips than I would have received from serving civilian passengers, but it also meant less pressure and less embarrassment because of my inexperience.

Before sailing, I had convinced myself, as many believe, that seasickness was purely psychological. When the sea became rough two days out, I had a real psychological battle on my hands. I won, however, by following the advice of an older, veteran seaman: Eat something immediately. The way I felt, eating something was the last thing I wanted to do. But in desperation, I took his advice and managed to eat a sandwich. To my amazement, it worked. I never have experienced seasickness since that day.

Before docking in Germany, the vessel routinely stopped in Southampton, England, to allow U.S. Air Force personnel and their dependents to disembark. Near the English Channel we could see the masts of four ships that had been sunk during World War II. At that time our pay was automatically increased to "hazardous duty" pay because of danger from leftover mines in these waters. This was fine with me; it meant more money for school.

We arrived in Germany at Bremerhaven. To me, Bremerhaven represented a cross section of postwar Germany. There were many partly bombed buildings where people lived in the wreckage. I noticed that a majority of the men still wore parts of old uniforms. As I got around, I definitely found it easier to speak German in Germany than in the classroom. When bartering with merchants, I often found a small audience gathered around, observing and noting my mistakes.

It was fortunate for me that the ship had to remain in port in Germany for a couple extra days before loading up for its return trip. Taking advantage of the free time, I took a train to Hamburg to visit some acquaintances. While enroute, I had to change trains in Bremen. As I was sightseeing during the wait, I stumbled on a statue of "The Town Musicians of Bremen." This was an interesting coincidence because in one of my German classes we had translated the story of *Die Stadt Musikanten von Bremen*.

The family I visited in Hamburg consisted of a father, mother, two daughters, and three sons. One daughter was a student at a college in Indiana near Fort Wayne. One daughter was a *Kranken-schwester* (literally, "sister of the sick")—a nurse. Unfortunately, the one son who was fluent in English was mountain climbing with friends. This resulted in some frustrating and mentally fatiguing days for me. To communicate, I had to think, repeat, rephrase, and repronounce what I was trying to express in German.

I ate dinner with the family and over black bread, soup, cheese, coffee, and cake, we had an interesting conversation. One thing I asked was how the German national anthem was sung. At that time, shortly after the war, the German people had no anthem. However, before this family would sing their former national anthem, they took certain precautions. They carefully scanned the area outside their house, then they tightly closed the windows. They had to be certain no one could hear them because singing *Deutschland Über Alles* in 1950 was *Verboten*. Anyone doing so could be reported to the authorities. After all their preparations, and with the windows tightly closed, this family softly gave me their rendition of *Deutschland Über Alles*.

I do not remember exactly what I gave to this family as souvenirs of the United States. Among the items they gave to me were some Nazi postage stamps, some Hitler Youth children's booklets, and a miniature basket with a handle, which was made from *Heide*, a unique plant that can live for more than 12 months without water.

In all these things I was like any other tourist, black or white. But as a Christian, I was puzzled that this family had no religious faith, no belief in God or in Jesus Christ. All the houses on their side of the street had been destroyed by bombs from air raids except their house. Likewise on the opposite side of the street only one building remained. When I asked if they believed that it might be by God's doing that only their dwelling and their lives had been spared, this family's response was no. To them no God existed. I could only think about how good and gracious God is to His creatures, even when they do not acknowledge Him.

The return voyage was for the most part uneventful, except for a day or so of storms and high waves. Back in New York City, I expressed gratitude and farewells to the Sabourins and left them with souvenirs from Germany. Then it was back to the "Bunk" in Fort Wayne, as we affectionately called Concordia Junior College. I had been blessed by God to have experienced lessons and practice in German that my classmates had not had. I was ready to complete my final year of prep school before enrolling at Concordia Seminary in St. Louis. I was getting closer to my goal of becoming a Lutheran pastor. My heart was full of thanksgiving to our gracious God for providing for me in such a marvelous way.

6

MY SECOND JOB
AS A SEAMAN

As I looked forward to enrolling at Concordia Seminary in St. Louis, there was another obstacle before me: finances. My dad's limited income as a custodian at the post office in St. Louis meant he could not help me. Nor could my mom's income from working as a domestic provide much support. For a black man to find a part-time job that paid a decent salary in St. Louis in the fall of 1950 was almost impossible. I certainly had no influential contacts to assist me.

The only logical solution I could think of to solve my dilemma was to take a year off to work at the best-paying job I had ever had. It meant going back to sea for a year. When my father heard of my plans, he didn't seem fazed. He had never been too keen on my decision to spend the necessary years in school to become a

Lutheran pastor. After moving his family to St. Louis from Mississippi, he had encouraged his brother to come also. One of his brother's sons became a dean at Lincoln University in Jefferson City, Missouri. Another became a doctor in St. Louis. Thus the only words of advice I received from my dad were, "Why don't you study something like my brother's boys so you can make some money? Why don't you become a doctor or a professor?" Later, however, my dad was proud to see me ordained in the service of the Lord as a Lutheran pastor.

With my mother it was a different story. When she heard of my decision to delay my enrollment at Concordia Seminary, she, as well as her friends and fellow church members, frantically tried to persuade me to give up the idea of working for a year. They were fearful that if I began to earn a good salary working aboard ship, I would give up the idea of becoming a Lutheran pastor. However, they offered no alternatives. What they did not understand was that I had received this strong inner feeling, this conviction, this "calling" to serve God as a pastor at an early age. Even as a child I used to turn my black raincoat around backward to serve as my cassock while I imitated my pastor, preaching to—or at—some of my playmates or stuffed animals. I was determined to be a pastor, with God's help.

After weathering the storms of protest, I returned to New York City and the Crewing Section in Brooklyn. By God's doing, I was sure, I was assigned to the same ship with much of the same crew as the previous summer—the *General George W. Goethals*.

In those days, a ship usually remained in port in Germany for only two or three days while it was unloaded and reloaded. Then it would head back to Brooklyn, arriving in about nine or ten days. Many of the crew spent their time and money with the women of ill repute who can be found in all port cities throughout the world. By God's grace I did more constructive things, visiting Lutheran churches, going to German movies, and attending operas or concerts. Once in the city of Hamburg I attended a presentation of Handel's *Messiah.*

One of the few opportunities I had to attend a church service that year was when I visited a pastor and his family in Hamburg. This pastor was a relative of Rev. Dr. Carl Zorn, who for a long time had served as secretary of the Atlantic District of The Lutheran Church—Missouri Synod, which had its offices in New York City. At the same time Rev. Zorn served a congregation in Closter, New Jersey.

The parish where I worshiped was located in a *Vorstadt*, or suburb, of Hamburg. When the cab driver let me out, at first I didn't see a church—at least not the church building I had expected to see. Instead, there was a small band playing hymns. The "church edifice," in front of which the little band played, was a low building with a flat roof. The structure was about half my height. To enter, one had to go down a few steps. When the service began, the band came inside. The organist played a pump organ, alternating stanzas with the band so he could rest.

Before the invocation, the pastor took his seat at one side of the altar. It happened to be the beginning of the school year, and each boy and girl of the new confirmation class came forward individually to curtsy or bow reverently before the pastor and recite a Scripture passage. Although I didn't catch everything, my German had improved enough that I learned something about the troubles of that congregation from the sermon. The gist of it was that during World War I their house of worship had been destroyed. *Alles war kaput!* By the grace of God, they had rebuilt. Then during World War II, their church building had been destroyed again. Only the basement had been left. But this congregation was determined, with God's help, to rebuild again.

The pastor, a man in his 80s, was elated to receive my greetings from his relatives in the United States. He also let me know how happy he was that I could worship with him and his congregation. He insisted that I come home with him for Sunday dinner, and he apologized after dinner that he could not remain home to visit with me, though he had a God-pleasing reason for his absence. This pastor had a tight schedule to keep to travel some distance to conduct another service that afternoon for a vacant congregation. Here was an example of true Christian charity and love from a Lutheran pastor. The fact that I was black meant nothing. I was a fellow Lutheran, and he welcomed me. That's the kind of pastor I meant to become.

One time when our vessel remained in port an extra couple of days, I had a chance to visit the city of Worms (or as the Germans say, "Vormss"), where Martin Luther had made his bold stand in defense of the Gospel. In the town square of Worms were several statues of former city fathers. The area around those statues was neatly maintained. In an adjacent area were statues of notables from the Reformation, such as Martin Luther and Philip Melanchthon. There the lawn was weedy and in need of cutting. I made an effort to ask some locals the reason behind the discrepancy in appearance. They told me what should have been obvious. The government was responsible for maintaining the area surrounding the one set of statues, and the church was responsible for maintaining the other. However, the church did not have any money.

It became amusing when I received feedback later from some of the people to whom I had sent picture postcards during my travels. One high school classmate described her puzzlement upon receiving my card that mentioned something about a "diet of worms." She wondered why people had been eating worms. Margaret's religious background was obviously not Lutheran nor was she a student of the Reformation.

Only one time was our layover in Southampton extended long enough so crew members could visit London. I looked in vain for a Lutheran church, which the local constables kept referring to as a "Lutherian church." I finally gave up and had as good a tour of London as possible with a taxi driver serving as guide. I saw the guards at Buckingham Palace before heading for Piccadilly Circus enroute to the train station. I was sight-seeing alone because, as is generally the case, most merchant seaman or sailors did not prefer to spend their free time in the companionship of someone who wants to become a minister.

At Piccadilly the stores had closed but the lights were still on in the display windows. As I paused in front of one window, examining the styles of the men's suits, an attractive young woman began to move, window by window, closer to where I stood. I suspected that, at close to 11 P.M., she was not going to invite me, a perfect stranger, to her house for tea and crumpets. Lord, have mercy! Just then one of London's finest, who was standing a few feet away, sized up the situation and, with one hand on his baton, turned toward the woman and bellowed: "Move along there, ya wench, a'fore I bop ya one!" Thus that temptation was removed quickly. With the help of the Lord, with His Word and promises on my mind, and with the aid of that English bobby, I was able to catch the last train to Southampton and get to my ship in good time.

Promotion

One of the highlights of my time on the ship was my promotion to petty officer. There had been another young man who served as a yeoman for the Steward Department. A yeoman in the navy is a petty officer who serves as a secretary or clerk. He happened to be an African American. There were constant rumors that he was a Communist because he read a great deal of the time. He also frequently spoke of the injustice and the indignities that black people had to endure throughout the United States and the world. He always went off alone when the ship was in port. Some thought he was attending Communist cell meetings. It was rumored that he was being investigated by the CIA. Whether he voluntarily left the ship's service or was removed as a result of some investigation, we never knew. (I believed that he was an intelligent, studious young man who was interested in history; however, he seemed to have grown discouraged and embittered about how his black brothers were treated in society.) I do know that his departure gave me an opportunity to advance in job status and pay.

When the second steward learned that I knew how to type, he encouraged me to apply for the yeoman's position. After the ship tied up in Brooklyn, I was given a typing test that I passed with flying colors. After a brief interview, and with recommendations, I was granted the conditional approval to fill the yeoman's position aboard ship. However, there was one catch. My seaman's papers had to be updated to endorse me as eligible to work at sea as a yeoman.

It was a day of vindication and triumph for me when I went back to the New York City Coast Guard station to have my seaman's papers upgraded. I arrived a little past 4:30 P.M., when the duty day ended. The only man present was the duty officer who was responsible for manning the station after hours in case of emergencies. He was an African American petty officer. When I told him why I had come, he said to come in and he would take care of me.

I considered this a God-blessed day. I talked with this Coastguardsman about my advancement and why no black personnel seemed to qualify as ordinary seamen or for work in the Engine Department, but only in the Steward Department. He said he didn't know. But when I later looked at my seaman's papers that he had updated, I was flabbergasted. He had endorsed me for employment at sea in all the following categories:

Waiter (fh) [food handler]

Ordinary Seaman [for work in Deck Department]

Wiper [for work in Engine Department]

Yeoman (any department) [for work as clerk]

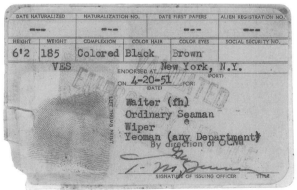

Although this battered document is now more than 50 years old, it is among my most treasured possessions, reminding me of the personal sense of triumph I felt that day. Yet I was aware that my victory over the racist practices of some of the white Coast-guardsmen was ironically the result of the bigotry of a Coast-guardsman of my own race. It did nothing to help other black or minority applicants who followed me. Still, I saw that God was looking after me. Not bad for a guy who, a year before, couldn't even set the table!

Employment as a yeoman meant, of course, that I would wear the khaki uniform of a U.S. Navy petty officer during duty hours aboard ship, eat in the dining salon like the other ship's officers, have different living quarters, and receive an increase in pay.

I counted the change in my living quarters as a blessing. No longer would I be forced to suffer the effects of having a room-mate who rarely took a shower. Some readers may remember a popular underarm deodorant called "Mum." The crewman who slept in the bunk beneath mine was given the nickname "Mums 'em Down" because that was what he would say when asked whether he planned to take a shower. Each time his reply would be: "Naw, I'm just gonna 'Mums 'em down.'" His daily routine, however, did not prevent me from mine: shower, read God's Word, and read my *Portals of Prayer* devotional booklet.

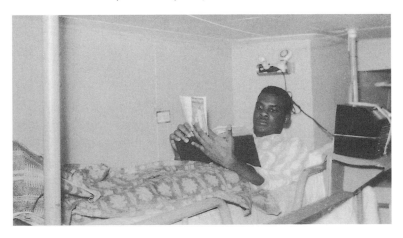

As a yeoman, my duties included cutting stencils and producing menus each day for the dining salon passengers, filling out requisition forms for supplies for the Steward Department, and so forth. My experience from making several voyages as a yeoman led to one other "day of triumph" before I concluded my year's service.

There was a section known as the Supply Department aboard each vessel of the transport fleet. The department included a supply officer, an assistant supply officer, and one or two yeomen. On the ship to which I had been assigned at the time, the supply officer was a white Protestant and the assistant supply officer was Jewish. The supply officer was openly anti-Semitic, which openly offended the assistant supply officer. The supply officer was sending advance messages to the Crewing Section in Brooklyn as we approached the city that he urgently had to have a replacement for his assistant. Meanwhile, the assistant supply officer was also sending frantic messages to the Crewing Section that he would need to be assigned to a different ship when we reached port.

According to the responses that the supply officer received, his hopes of replacing his assistant immediately seemed pretty slim. The Crewing Section's continued response was that it lacked qualified personnel to fill the position of assistant supply officer if the individual currently holding that position should be relieved.

When we reached port, the assistant supply officer was notified that he had been promoted to the position of supply officer, though on a smaller ship. Although a day of victory for this man, in a sense, it was also a day of triumph for me because the Crewing Section officials decided the only available candidate was a black individual whom they had deemed qualifiable if not already qualified. And that black individual was me.

When I was informed that I was to be the new assistant supply officer, I had some apprehension. Having found fault with his previous assistant primarily because the man was a Jew, how would the supply officer deal with a black man? Also I had some concern about my lack of experience in the particular duties of the assistant supply officer's job, but I was always willing to learn new ways of doing things. After prayer and with trust in God, I accepted the position.

What a day it must have been for the anti-Semitic supply officer. He got rid of his Jewish assistant only to have him immediately replaced by an inexperienced black assistant. There was a lot that he could say, but nothing that he could do about the situation. Although it was the beginning of August, I knew that with the seminary school year fast approaching, I would have only enough time to make one last trip to Germany. But I was elated to make the trip as a ship's officer. I had to buy new uniforms with epaulets on the shoulders of the jackets, just like U.S. Navy officers wore, but the pride and the prestige that went with the position made it worthwhile. And I had received another pay raise with the new position. Once again, God was my help in time of need.

After my final trip for the transport service, I sadly left the ship, the job, and the city of New York to return to St. Louis and my family. With the help of the Lord through His powerful Word, the adventure and the salary of my employment did not tempt me or cause me to abandon my goal to enter Concordia Seminary and pursue my God-given ambition to serve the Lord full-time as a Lutheran pastor. I was on my way at last.

7

SEMINARY
AND VICARAGE

During the fall of 1951, I enrolled at Concordia Seminary in Clayton, Missouri, a predominately white suburb of St. Louis. I knew that I would be struggling not only with my class work but also with the influences of racism in St. Louis County. Along with other seminary students, I was a resident of Clayton because I was living in a dormitory on the campus. It amused me to see how surprised, puzzled, and sometimes annoyed white people would be when they learned my address and discovered that it was not my employer's address. I did, in fact, live in Clayton.

Some of the seminary students regularly made use of the public swimming pool reserved for residents of Clayton. Occasionally I went with them, and we discovered that when the group of students were all white, they were admitted without question. Each time I was with them, everyone in the group was required to produce proof of residency. Before long we began to feel that this racist practice was perhaps for the purpose of compiling a list of everyone who was willing to swim with a black person in the Clayton pool. On more than one occasion I wondered how long it would be before black people could come and go in public places and walk or drive through any community without being regarded with suspicion or scorn.

During a holiday break in 1951, I agreed to substitute as a night watchman at a construction site for a classmate who wanted to go home to Pennsylvania. On my way to the job, I had to drive through a small municipality in St. Louis County. I drove carefully, right at the speed limit. Before long a municipal police car was all I could see in my rear view mirror, and the car stayed right behind me, turning when I turned, slowing down when I slowed. Eventually, the car passed me, then drove about five miles under the speed limit, increasing speed only when I tried to pass. We came to the top of a hill and started to descend. Because it was legal to exceed the speed limit when passing a car (on a two-lane road) and because I had to get to work, I passed the police car. No sooner was I back in the right-hand lane than the red lights began to flash and the siren to blare. I pulled to the side of the road, disgusted and angry.

Two police officers approached my car. One stood on the passenger side, pointing a pistol at me. The officer on the driver's side demanded my identification. We went through the routine I knew so well: "Yes, I live in Clayton. No, that is not the address of my employer." I was taken to the police station and charged with passing a car on a hill. The police chief exploded in anger at his officers when they verified my explanation that they were driving down the hill when I passed their car. Later, the seminary dean, Dean Wuerffel, used his influence and persuasion in a phone conversation with the police chief, and I was not required to return to answer a summons. The actions of those young officers were motivated by racism. Their suspicion of me, a black man who was driving through a white community, was the result of the racist environment in which these men lived and worked.

Despite continuing racial incidents, progress in human relations was being made in St. Louis County, though the changes were barely perceptible. When I left St. Louis for Fort Wayne in the mid-1940s, the white-owned drive-in restaurants would not serve food to black people, though they remained nearly out of sight in their cars. In the early 1950s, these same establishments gave black people the right to receive drive-in service along with the rest of the dining public. But there was a catch: The car had to be driven by a white person and the black customers had to be in the back seat.

This situation always presented a problem when I was driving my own car on a double date with a white classmate. Should my date and I move to the back seat of my car and the white couple move to the front? Should I bow to the dictates of racism for the convenience of being served food at a first-rate eating establishment near the dormitory? Should I, on the other hand, drive several miles to the ghetto where a person's race or nationality was never a factor? Would the day come when white and black customers would be served on an equal basis?

Things often were downright ridiculous. The Forest Park Highlands amusement park in St. Louis remained strictly whites only throughout my childhood until I was too old to care for such entertainment nor was I puzzled any longer by the system that allowed such injustice. All the movie theaters were closed to black people. The exceptions included four or five theaters located in the black community and two theaters that were permitted to show foreign films only if there was no policy of discrimination.

At the American Theater, black persons were admitted to the balcony only.

While at the seminary, a high school classmate told me that the theaters had changed their policy and black people were now permitted to attend midtown and downtown movie houses. Because of my studies, I could not take advantage of this new development immediately, but during the Christmas break, my roommate, Paul Erdman, and I planned an evening in town that included dinner and a movie. We went to the Fred Harvey restaurant in Union Station, the one place where we could both sit down and enjoy a good meal. After dinner we went to the Fox Theater on Grand Avenue. The cashier informed us that she could sell a ticket to Paul but not to me. I could not believe this, so I persuaded Paul to try the Missouri Theater. There we heard the same story. Paul and I drove downtown and tried once more, and once more we heard that white people could buy tickets, but black people could not. I did not understand how my friend could have given me such misleading information.

What we did not know was that the policy had been reversed because so many black people were coming that the owners were fearful the black community was going to take over "their" theaters. The real reason for the increased patronage was that the movie-projector operators in the black theaters had gone on strike and no movies were being shown in the black community.

Because Paul and I did not know the policy had changed, I persuaded him to try once more. Probably to demonstrate how ridiculous the system was, and perhaps to reinforce what I already knew, I asked Paul to go to another theater and perform a test. While I remained in the car, Paul asked the cashier if he could buy a ticket for a friend who was from North Korea. (At the time, the United States was engaged in the Korean War.) Paul returned to the car with the information that such a ticket could be bought.

That did it for me. I made up my mind then and there that I was going to the movies in St. Louis, and I was not going to wait too many years to do it.

Another classmate, Bob Wilson, went with me to a costume shop where I rented a turban with a fake emerald attached to the front. The idea was to wear the turban as a disguise to make me acceptable and eligible for admittance. There were four of us in the group that drove downtown to Loews Theater. Four tickets were purchased. The three white students and their "East Indian" friend walked into the theater without incident, took their seats, and enjoyed the movie.

All this I went through just to see a first-run movie without waiting five or six weeks for it to be shown in a black neighborhood theater. Was it worth all the trouble? No, not really, but it gave me a sense of triumph over the racist system that tolerated and accepted any race of humanity except native-born Americans who are black. Shortly after the turban incident, the foreign-made film *Martin Luther* was shown at Loews. I was told that this film could be shown only with the stipulation that there be no discrimination against the audience. When that film closed, the theater continued to admit mixed audiences, and other theaters began to follow suit.

Throughout my seminary days, I had to work at an outside job. While my classmates were hired by downtown banks or suburban clothing stores, I drove delivery cars for a drugstore chain or trucks for a grocery store. I made the foolish mistake of starting my first semester with a full-time job as a night porter at the Chase Park Plaza Hotel, working from 7 P.M. to 7 A.M. I went directly from work to my first class of the day—Hebrew. I did more nodding than paying attention to Professor George Schick. At the end of the first semester, I was one of the chosen few to flunk Hebrew. I could not seem to master the fundamentals of the language that is so essential for translating and studying the Old Testament. I was required to repeat the course until I did pass.

At about the time that grades were to be distributed, I received word that the seminary president, Dr. Louis Sieck, wanted to see me in his office. What could he want with me, I wondered. Was he singling me out as the only black member of a student body of some 400 future pastors? Had word reached him already that I was going to fail Hebrew? After some courteous small talk, I was relieved and somewhat surprised to learn that Dr. Sieck wanted to know how I was being treated on campus and whether I had been experiencing any problems from racism. I assured Dr. Sieck that I had no complaints of either faculty or students that stemmed from racial prejudice or discrimination. If racism was present on the campus, it was covert and suppressed in my presence.

Two or three days after this conversation, I found a book in the seminary bookstore written by a black Presbyterian pastor in Harlem, Dr. James Robinson. The book, *Road without Turning*, was a straightforward account of the vicious racial prejudice the author had encountered during his days at seminary. I did not know for sure, but I felt that the appearance of this book on our campus had something to do with my meeting with Dr. Sieck.

My troubles with the Hebrew language made me wonder if I would end up as a well-informed layman instead of a parish pastor. But I hung in there, successfully repeated Hebrew, and at last reached my year of vicarage. I was assigned to First Immanuel Lutheran Church in Chicago, Illinois, under the direction of Rev. Dr. Ralph Moellering. This good man combined the qualities of a parish pastor, a scholar, a prophet, and a missionary with vision and imagination. He also was a prolific writer.

Rev. Moellering wanted me assigned to his church on the near west side of Chicago in an area where people of various races and nationalities lived. In one section there was a Greek settlement, in another a Sicilian colony, and in another direction were black and Puerto Rican people and other ethnic groups living in public housing projects. The nucleus of the congregation was composed of people of German descent, many of whom had moved to the suburbs but returned to the church on Sunday for worship. Many of these individuals had been baptized, confirmed, and married in this church and their parents had been buried from this building. Pastor Moellering was also serving as campus pastor for the Lutheran students who were enrolled at some of the schools in the nearby Chicago Medical Center.

Pastor Moellering wanted a vicar to help him with outreach primarily to the minorities living in the public housing projects. When he first proposed this idea to the district's mission board, it was met with only mild approval. However, when it was learned that he had requested an additional subsidy to underwrite the expense of a black vicar, one member of the mission board expressed strong opposition to such an idea. The racist thinking of this man is revealed in what he said to Pastor Moellering: "It's all right to extend an invitation to those people but you don't have to send someone out to knock on doors to invite them. After all, they can hear the Gospel preached on the *Lutheran Hour*." (This is an international radio broadcast sponsored by the Lutheran Laymen's League of The Lutheran Church—Missouri Synod.)

Although Pastor Moellering met with criticism, he persisted and I was assigned to him as a vicar. I remained as his vicar longer than the usual one-year term. This did not happen until after some stormy sessions with the district's mission board. Pastor Moellering took an unbudging stand to share the Gospel of Jesus Christ with the minority people in his church's neighborhood. The board withdrew financial support but backpedaled when the congregation threatened to join the English District.

During my vicarage, from January 1955 until June 1956, there were no problems with racism within the congregation. I was authorized by the congregation to assist the pastor with the distribution of Holy Communion. Programs for the youth included various racial and ethnic groups. At one service I had the privilege of baptizing 25 children.

It was all too apparent, however, that racism was an influence in the Lutheran Church. Pastor Moellering and I attended a pastoral conference in a Chicago suburb where one venerable pastor presented a paper that attempted to demonstrate that segregation was compatible with the teachings of Christianity. That evening, Pastor Moellering began to write. And did he ever write! The next morning several volunteers and I distributed Pastor Moellering's rebuttal, a paper that was written on short notice but was scholarly, biblical, and supported by the Lutheran Confessions, to which all the Lutheran pastors subscribed.

I have never been able to understand how people can think it compatible with Christian beliefs purposely to set up artificial barriers between people based solely on race. Christ came to break down the "dividing wall of hostility" between Jew and Gentile (Ephesians 2:14). The same applies to white people and black.

There were two older black Lutheran pastors who impressed on me the idea that I could serve God full-time in the ministry and at the same time work for better human relations in the church and in society. One pastor was Rev. Sabourin, mentioned previously, who was for many years the president of the Lutheran Human Relations Association of America. The other pastor was Rev. Dr. Marmaduke Carter of St. Philip Lutheran Church in Chicago. He had a reputation for giving lectures and sermons in the German language. On one occasion, I asked Rev. Carter why he had started to preach in German. He said that when he was younger and went about preaching and lecturing on behalf of missions in black communities in the South, he visited many rural congregations in Nebraska, Iowa, and Kansas. He soon found that about the only words in English that most of the people understood were "corn" and "money." Consequently, he was forced to communicate with them in their own language—German.

One story illustrates both the dignity and sense of humor of Rev. Carter. At a pastor's conference Rev. Carter was on the platform along with other dignitaries. The master of ceremonies turned to him during the introductions and impulsively said, "Dr. Carter, won't you say something to us in German?" Thus this individual treated the distinguished pastor as if he were a performing dog. Instead of taking it as an insult, Rev. Carter drew himself up to his full height, walked in a slow and stately manner to the podium, leaned forward, and said in a deep voice, "Sauerkraut!" Then he returned slowly to his seat as the audience broke up with laughter and the embarrassed master of ceremonies looked around in bewilderment.

Because I was concerned about working for better human relations, I made a special effort to learn the German language well enough to conduct a Lutheran service. This particular accomplishment had been dropped from the list of requirements for graduation long before my days at the seminary, but there were still congregations that featured a German service on Sunday morning. Unlike the other languages we were required to study at the seminary—Latin, Greek, and Hebrew—German was a language that could be spoken to another person. I felt that if I could communicate with German-speaking people, I might be able to change some false thinking about black people.

8

WHITE CHRISTIANS AND A BLACK PASTOR

In June 1957, I graduated from Concordia Seminary, St. Louis, and was ordained as a pastor in The Lutheran Church—Missouri Synod. What a day of joy that was! My first assignment was a call to serve as a missionary of the Atlantic District. I was to make a door-to-door canvass in the Newark and Montclair areas of New Jersey. The survey was to ascertain the feasibility of organizing a new Lutheran congregation in one of those cities.

Because I did not have a regular place for preaching each Sunday, I was called on as guest preacher when other pastors in the area needed a substitute. During this time, I preached my first sermon in the German language, at a congregation in New Milford, New Jersey. The pastor was Rev. Ralph Zorn, and by a strange twist of fate, I preached for him again some years later, in

English, in a German congregation he served at that time in West Berlin. After conducting a German service, my name was added to the list of Atlantic District pastors who could handle services in English and German.

One day in 1958, I received a phone call from a man who identified himself as the president of a congregation in a remote area of New York. He said that their pastor was hospitalized and asked if I could conduct their English and German services the following Sunday, Palm Sunday. The caller promised to send me a map with directions to their community. As an afterthought, he asked if I would return on Maundy Thursday to conduct the Communion service. The caller suggested that I meet him at the parsonage, then after the services we would have dinner at a restaurant on the parkway leading back to New York City.

A few days later I received a letter from this man that included a detailed map. In addition he had enclosed a card on which was printed a quotation from a speech attributed to Abraham Lincoln. It said in part, "I would never want to see a black man become a juror or marry a white woman. . . . This card should be placed in the hands of all teachers, social workers, ministers, etc." The card was from the Gerald L. K. Smith Group, a well-known racist organization. I asked myself why the president of the congregation had sent this card to me. I was apprehensive and considered canceling.

On Palm Sunday morning I found my way to the church and to the parsonage, where I met the congenial wife of the pastor. The president of the congregation did not appear, so I had a word of prayer for the pastor and went on to the church. As I was waiting in my car, the president of the congregation arrived. I feared he would have a serious attack of apoplexy when he saw my white clerical collar and my black face. I saw immediately that he had not known beforehand that I was black. I thanked him for the excellent directions. He recovered his composure and, excusing himself, went across the road to the home of one of the officers of the congregation. He was back in a few minutes, and with an air of relaxed confidence he said, "Well, you won't have to worry about coming back here on Maundy Thursday. We have that all worked out."

I went into the church and conducted first the English and then the German service. When the second service was concluded and I had finished greeting the worshipers at the door, the president came up to me. I took it as a real compliment when he said that as he was returning to the church, the worshipers kept stopping to shake his hand because they thought he was personally responsible for arranging for me to conduct the service, and they were pleased and grateful. I was then told of a change in dinner plans. We were to have dinner at his home because his mother-in-law had suddenly become ill and he did not want to leave her alone. I understood his predicament. A man of his conviction and evidently of his reputation could hardly afford to be seen in a local restaurant on a Sunday afternoon with a black man. The conversation at the dinner table was interesting as he talked about his dairy farm and his opinion on breeding cattle. He was persistent in his emphasis that if a certain type of bull should inadvertently be allowed to breed with the wrong kind of cow, then "you got nothing." I got the point.

While the German-speaking members of this congregation accepted me, I wondered if my efforts to better human relations through my use of the German language would be of any help at all to the clergy. I attended a local Lutheran pastoral conference, and after the business session, the pastors had lunch together. One of them asked me to conduct services for him three weeks later because I could handle a German service. I agreed, and he gave me the information I needed. Then the pastor continued his conversation with the other pastors at the table. One pastor who served in Secaucus, New Jersey, was speaking about the distasteful odors from the packing house, odors to which one had to become accustomed when living in a certain section of that city. The same pastor who had asked me to substitute for him responded by saying, "Well, I'll tell you one thing, if you think the stench is bad in Secaucus, you ought to smell how the niggers stink in Newark."

I was speechless. This man had been serving as a Christian pastor for years, yet he had an ingrained racist attitude. He was typical of many pastors of all Christian denominations who were nurtured and supported by a racist society, by racist teachers, by racist colleagues, and by influential racist laypeople. They all believed, contrary to the Gospel of Jesus Christ, that racism and Christianity are compatible.

The Chaplaincy

While at seminary, I had become interested in the military chaplaincy because we had several reserve chaplains teaching courses at that time who influenced me. One was Rev. Dr. Arthur Carl Piepkorn, who retired as a full colonel and at one time had served as commandant of the U.S. Army Chaplains School. Another professor was Rev. Dr. Martin H. Scharlemann, who became the first U.S. Air Force Reserve chaplain to be promoted to brigadier general. The others were Prof. Harry G. Coiner and Prof. Phillip Schroeder.

When I graduated from the seminary, I had received the endorsement of the Armed Forces Commission of The Lutheran Church—Missouri Synod, the first step in becoming a chaplain. The next step was to find an Army Reserve or National Guard unit whose commanding officer would grant approval for assignment to a vacancy in his unit.

While I was serving as a missionary pastor for the Atlantic District, I investigated the possibilities for a chaplain's assignment in that area. I went to Governor's Island to the Army Area Head-quarters, where I was given a list of units that had vacancies to be filled by a Protestant chaplain. One of these was the Infantry Division of the New Jersey National Guard. I called and made an appointment for an interview.

In my interview, I was asked about my qualifications. I was asked if I knew the other black chaplain in the New Jersey National Guard. I was asked whether he had sent me to inquire about this vacant slot. Both questions I answered in the negative. I was asked about my position on the NAACP, and I was proud to say I had been a card-carrying member since my student days in St. Louis. The interviewer then went into a tirade about the good old days before the NAACP had interfered, when the whites had their guard units and "coloreds" had their units. When this monologue was finished, I asked the chaplain if I would send his recommendation to the commanding officer so I could be commissioned. I was then told about the possibility of a reorganization of commands in this division and the possibility that the Protestant chaplain slot would be eliminated. This man didn't want me to buy all those uniforms for nothing. I explained that I intended to spend at least twenty years in the chaplaincy and could use the uniforms in some other unit if necessary.

Needless to say, I never made it into the New Jersey National Guard, but this was only the beginning of a series of encounters with racism in my attempts to be commissioned as a chaplain. I began systematically to make appointments with the commanding officers of every unit on the list I had received from the Army Reserves Chaplains' Office. The first unit needed a "Jewish" chaplain; the second unit needed a "Roman Catholic" chaplain. I called the Chaplains' Office, thinking that the information was out of date, but I was assured that the information on vacant slots in the various reserve and guard units was accurate.

After several more visits to units where I was not even given an interview, I was ready to recruit the assistance of the NAACP. But first I met the commanding officer of the 37th General Hospital Army Reserve Unit in Jamaica, Long Island, New York. I believe God led me to this interview with Colonel Dorman, a surgeon and a fine Christian gentleman. He told me that he had interviewed several other men for the position and wanted a little more time before coming to a decision. In the meantime, he asked if I would come to the next Sunday drill assembly of the unit and conduct a brief Protestant service. At the time, I was living in New York and serving as assistant pastor on the staff of St. John the Evangelist Lutheran Church in the Williamsburg section of Brooklyn. To comply with Colonel Dorman's request presented no problem. I conducted that first service and shortly after was recommended for the chaplain's post.

It had taken almost a year to be approved for this position, and I looked forward to securing my commission and beginning my career as a first lieutenant in the chaplain branch of the U.S. Army Reserves. Then I was informed that because of the time that had elapsed, I would have to request another endorsement from the Armed Forces Commission of The Lutheran Church—Missouri Synod. One of the members of the commission told me that when my name was considered, another member objected because "Sam Hoard will use the military chaplaincy to promote the cause of integration." Rev. Dr. Arthur Weber, a commission member and a friend, assured the commission that he knew me personally and that I would be an asset to the church and to the chaplaincy.

Interracial Parish Ministry

In 1960, about the same time I was approved as a chaplain, I accepted a call to serve as co-pastor in the interracial ministry at Our Savior Lutheran Church in Brooklyn. In this congregation of about 280 communicant members, there were only three or four black Lutherans. But the population in the community was rapidly doubling, and the newcomers were for the most part black and Puerto Rican.

Pastor Ralph Egolf wanted a racially integrated ministry in the chancel so people would know without a doubt that the congregation was serious when it proclaimed a welcome to all and its interest in a racially integrated membership in the pews. After about year, Pastor Egolf accepted a call in upstate New York, and in the few months that elapsed before another pastor was installed, I had the full responsibility of serving the congregation. The nucleus of the congregation, most of them elderly people with German backgrounds, accepted my ministry without reservation.

Only one member expressed his displeasure because I visited him in his home. He thought that my ministry was to be directed only to the minority people in the community. His problem was further complicated when he saw me in my chaplain's uniform. "Well," he said, "you're a lieutenant. When I was in the service, I was only a sergeant." The following Sunday after worship, as people were leaving the church, I heard someone say, "That was a nice sermon, Sam." I thought surely that one of my former classmates was at the service because no one in this congregation had ever called me anything but "Pastor." The voice I heard was that of the disgruntled parishioner. Because of his strong ties with the church in the past, he could not bring himself to transfer his membership. Because of his strong conditioning in racist concepts, he could not accept my ministry. To him I was almost a layman. Eventually, he solved his dilemma by transferring to another congregation.

When the new white pastor, Rev. William Puder, joined me, we planned our work so for about thirty days at a time one pastor was responsible for all weddings, Baptisms, and funerals. The congregation did not know exactly when we would change places. We wanted members of the congregation to know and to accept the full ministry of both pastors without prejudice.

Pastor Puder, who was fluent in English and Spanish, geared his ministry primarily toward the Spanish-speaking individuals and families moving into the community. He was instrumental in beginning classes in English and building bridges of goodwill in other ways to the Spanish-speaking people in the community. He was on the verge of beginning services in the Spanish when he accepted a call to the Midwest.

9

MINISTRY
IN THE CITY

Jesus said, "I am the good shepherd; I know My sheep . . . and I lay down My life for the sheep." (John 10:14–15). Through the prophets, it is said of the Lord, "He who scattered Israel will gather them and will watch over His flock like a shepherd" (Jeremiah 31:10). And again the Bible tells us: "He tends His flock like a shepherd" (Isaiah 40:11). St. Paul in his farewell sermon to the Lord's followers at Ephesus said: "Keep watch over yourselves and all the flock of which the Holy Spirit has made you overseers. Be shepherds of the church of God, which He bought with His own blood" (Acts 20:28). St. Peter said: "Be shepherds of God's flock that is under your care, serving as overseers—not because you must, but because you are willing, as God wants you to be" (1 Peter 5:2). Jesus emphasized to Peter how much He wanted

His followers to tend to His flock when He said not once, not twice, but three times: "Feed My lambs"; "Take care of My sheep"; "Feed My sheep" (John 21:15–17). Many think this means providing only spiritual care for the members of the flock. However, when it comes to showing concern for the physical needs of the flock, many of us fall short. We seem to feel that this does not apply to shepherds of the flock in our day.

David, like other shepherds, carried a studded club, almost three feet long, to protect his flock against predators. He also had a slingshot, like the one with which he slew Goliath. With it he could fell a marauding wolf or bear, a jackal or lion. Like sheep, members of the flock today need a good shepherd to protect them, to be advocates for them, and to protest with them against predators in society.

Jesus the Good Shepherd had compassion on the people because they were "harassed and helpless like sheep without a shepherd" (Matthew 9:36). How did the image of the Good Shepherd fit with my ministry in the city? People there were harassed and made to suffer pain and harm, both mental and physical.

For example, in 1959 when I first began serving in the interracial ministry at Our Savior Lutheran Church in Brooklyn, the congregation had only three nonwhite families, including my own. However, the formerly all-white neighborhood was rapidly becoming racially integrated and at the same time more crowded. Many of the older white members recalled that in their earlier years anytime someone heard hammering or sawing in an adjacent apartment, a city inspector would quickly arrive to see if any code violations had been committed. Now things were different. In the past, city officials saw to it that the three-story apartment buildings on the block, each of which contained six separate apartments, stayed that way. But now apartment owners were being allowed to convert what had been single-family apartment units into two-family units by adding an additional bathroom and a kitchenette. Thus what had been a six-family apartment unit suddenly became a more lucrative 12-family building with an absentee landlord.

As the neighborhood became more crowded, the problems of living in the community grew. More people meant fewer opportunities for getting to know others as neighbors. These abnormally crowded living conditions resulted in a growing lack of concern for the rights of others: Loud music played on weekends; a growing number of disputes between neighbors occurred; people were careless with trash. These things caused pain to those who were accustomed to living orderly lives and keeping their buildings neat and clean.

The Work of the Shepherd

Could I, as pastor of the church in the middle of the block, do or say anything that might make a difference? With God's help, I was taking care of the spiritual nourishment of the flock through the traditional Sunday worship services and festivals of the church

year. We had a Wednesday evening Bible class that averaged around 35 in attendance. This included a few teenagers and young adults, as well as senior citizens—all attracted to the Word of God but possibly also by the coffee and *Küchen*. Of course, I was regularly taking the Sacrament to the shut-ins and hospitalized and seeking out the delinquents.

But what could I do to help alleviate the pain of the members and those we were striving to reach? To me, it seemed that we needed to develop a sense of community among the people on our block. For people living in New York City, this was no easy task. From Monday to Friday, most people would leave their apartments in the morning, walk to Broadway Avenue, and take the subway into the city. They would return from work in the evening the same way. There was no chitchat with neighbors across the fence. There was no yard. There was no social interaction with the people living on the third floor or the second floor, except maybe in passing in the hallway. There were no social concerns discussed with the people across the street. To develop a sense of community under these circumstances was no easy task.

Several families suggested forming a block club. They were genuinely interested and assisted in persuading others come to an organizational meeting at the church. The results of our efforts were some neat and professionally produced signs, which were affixed to fences or beside stoops of certain houses along the block. The signs read: "Curb Your Dog," "Please Don't Litter," "Help Keep Our Neighborhood Clean." We were able to get the cooperation of several families on the block to underwrite the cost of the signs. These efforts helped.

The Rochdale Protest

Rochdale Village was a huge complex of middle-income apartments being erected in the early to mid-1960s in Queens. It would end up with its own post office, a food court, and various shops and businesses all within the complex. However, at the time when its initial construction began, minorities were not hired as construction workers on the project. This caused pain in all the community, including among members of my flock. Federal dollars were being used to finance the building of Rochdale—dollars attached to laws that stated no discrimination was allowable in hiring practices. But qualified black individuals and those of other minority groups were not even considered for positions as, let alone hired as, plumbers, electricians, brick layers, painters, etc.

A committee of several community leaders tried in vain to negotiate with the contractors to get them to obey the law and follow fair practices in the hiring process. The contractors blamed the unions as the source of the problem. The union leaders claimed that the contractors were the cause of the problem. Among the community leaders involved in the negotiations were the head of the local NAACP chapter in Queens (William Booth, an attorney who later became a judge in Queens) and the head of the local chapter of the Committee of Racial Equality (CORE). In an effort to focus public attention on the unfair situation, these leaders sent calls throughout the city for assistance from concerned individuals. What were pastors to do when they received a call to help? Many did not or could not respond to the call. However, Rev. Edwin Thompson, pastor of Trinity Lutheran Church of Locust Manor, and I were two pastors of The Lutheran Church—Missouri Synod who did respond.

Because Trinity was close to the site where construction was beginning on Rochdale Village, Rev. Thompson made arrangements for the leaders and participants of the civil-rights demonstrations to meet at his church. Each day we met for instructions on expected conduct while on the picket lines. We also discussed any progress being made in our negotiations before going to the construction site to begin our demonstrations. The picket lines that we set up at the site each day eventually led to the voluntary arrest of many of us involved in the demonstrations.

The volunteers consisted of individuals drawn from the membership roles of organizations such as the NAACP and CORE, plus housewives and shiftworkers who would picket with us for a few hours before or after work. Some protesters were postal workers, store clerks, or self-employed individuals. Some were from the ranks of the unemployed, and some came from various churches. Among the clergymen who participated, Rev. Thompson and I were the only ones who regularly wore our clerical collars.

Our demonstrations at Rochdale Village had the following goals:

- To make people in the community aware of the injustice of the situation.
- To embarrass and get positive action out of the government officials who had the responsibility for enforcing the civil-rights laws.
- To persuade the contractors and union officials to comply voluntarily with the laws as an alternative to our hindering their jobs by picketing.

How well I remember Rev. Thompson and me marching and singing "We Shall Overcome," "Amen," "Ain't Nobody Gonna Turn Me 'Roun'," and some of the other civil-rights songs of the day as we held our protest signs high enough to be sure passersby or representatives of the press could plainly see what our protests were all about. The Borough of Queens police officials supervised our demonstrations. A high-ranking police official in his white-shirted uniform (a superintendent, I believe) was always on hand while we picketed. All the other police officers on duty at the scene were in plain clothes.

For some reason there was only one entry road by which the

cement trucks, lumber trucks, and other vehicles could enter the construction premises. The police superintendent allowed our picket line to march back and forth and block all traffic trying to enter this roadway for about 15 minutes. Then he would say, "Okay, your time's up," and he would allow the supply trucks to have access for about 15 minutes. However, those of us who were in the middle of the roadway at the time our picket line was cut off would deliberately walk slower and slower. Some of us would eventually plop down in the middle of the dusty roadway. Then a nonuniformed police officer would come over and say to each individual on the ground three times: "You will have to move or I will have to place you under arrest." With this routine, we were able to delay the delivery of needed construction materials for more than our allotted time. Of course, sometimes a picketer opted to remain positioned on the ground until he was arrested. This delayed the trucks even longer and gave publicity to our protest for justice.

In our morning meetings, anyone planning or willing to be arrested on that day would make this desire known to Bill Booth. He in turn would coordinate events so the media would know in advance the approximate time of the protest and the number of persons willing to be arrested. He also would notify the proper NAACP personnel so lawyers would be prepared to bail protesters out of jail, either that evening or the next morning.

This protest took place in the mid-1960s, and I remember Bill Booth possessing one of the smallest cameras I had ever seen. It was no more than 7 or 8 inches long and no more than about 2-1/2 inches wide. As people were being ushered to the paddy wagon by the police, Booth was nearly always on hand, his camera at the ready, saying, "All right, now, let's not be manhandling our people. I have my camera on you!" And needless to say, no one was ever roughed up.

When Rev. Thompson and I were arrested, my picture appeared on the front page of the *Long Island Press* between the arms of two police officers who were about to put me into a paddy wagon. On the Sunday morning after my arrest, a white teenage member of my church pulled me aside and said rather disappointedly, "We've been seeing all the pictures of the people getting arrested in the civil-rights demonstrations, and we looked in the paper and there was *your* picture!" After church I found it necessary to review with him the need for the civil-rights demonstrations and voluntary arrests.

Being in a jail in Queens overnight was not difficult, especially when it was voluntary and done as part of an effort to fight injustice. We were bonded out on our own recognizance by NAACP attorneys, and our cases were constantly postponed until the judge finally threw them out. Our work paid off. After continuous negotiations with contractors and union officials, fair hiring practices were initiated for the construction project and, thanks to our Lord's help, we were able to call off our demonstrations with a feeling of satisfaction and success.

Taking on the Schools

The "Allen Plan" was cause for additional civil-rights demonstrations by clergymen acting in the role of good shepherds. The plan caused harm to the children of various flocks in the city of New York because of the rampant racial segregation in the public schools. School papers were being marked "Excellent" when the kids could not even spell their names correctly. Minority youngsters who were functionally illiterate were being graduated from junior high school. Having suffered from an inferior education in segregated St. Louis public schools, I felt deeply about this issue.

Rev. Milton Galamison was pastor of a large Presbyterian church in Brooklyn and an outspoken civil-rights activist. He had initiated the idea of having inner-city youngsters boycott the public schools and attend "Freedom Schools" at his church and various other churches. The intent of Rev. Galamison's plan was not only to alleviate the problem of inner-city pupils not learning but also to spur school officials to action by hitting them in the pocketbook. It was no secret that for every day a child was absent, the monies allocated for the school budget based on attendance were cut.

Dr. Calvin E. Gross was superintendent of the school system in 1964 when a blue-ribbon committee was appointed to study the situation and develop a plan to alleviate the problems and improve the education system. Among those on the committee were a scholar of the Jewish faith, another of the Roman Catholic faith, and the chairman, Dr. Allen. This group proposed a plan that would improve the integration of the school system and would require minimal busing. Because Dr. Allen was chairman of the committee, the plan became known as the "Allen Plan." Everybody knew the plan had been completed and submitted to Superintendent Gross in ample time for him to implement before the next term. However, Superintendent Gross allowed the plan to lie dormant the entire summer.

An ad hoc committee was formed of Baptist, Methodist, Presbyterian, Lutheran, and other denominational clergy. Besides myself, some of the Lutheran pastors on the committee included Rev. John E. Puelle and Rev. Richard John Neuhaus, who had begun a "Freedom School" at St. John the Evangelist Lutheran Church in Brooklyn, where I had once served as assistant pastor. The result of this meeting was that as many pastors as possible were contacted to support the picketing of the New York City school-board offices, which were located in downtown Brooklyn. Each morning when school-board employees and others arrived for work, they saw ministers surrounding the block, silently picketing holding up signs that read: "Adopt the Allen Plan," "Integrate the Schools," and "When Will You Adopt the Allen Plan?" We also had a Roman Catholic priest, one of the notorious Berrigan brothers, join our picket line for a few days. He and his brother had become well known for trespassing on government property as they sought justice in various causes.

After picketing for several mornings, we decided to give our demonstration a more dramatic turn by holding a sit-in in Superintendent Gross's office. This would bring attention to our cause, and, we hoped, some positive action as a result. When we first entered Dr. Gross's office, he was in another part of the building. Our complement was 14 ministers strong. When Dr. Gross returned to his office, he asked us to leave and let him use his office. He said there was another office upstairs that we could occupy so as not to prevent him from getting his work done. One of our spokesmen pointed out that he had had several months to get work done on the Allen Plan but had done nothing.

Repeatedly Dr. Gross said we were to leave his office or he would have no alternative but to call the police to remove us. But he did not want to do this to a group of ministers. By now reporters were gathering in the hallways. They were not allowed to enter the office where we were. Just prior to the noon hour, our ranks were thinned by ministers who pleaded that they had urgent business to take care of at church. "But I'll be back to join you later," they all said. Of course the doors had been secured and anyone leaving was not allowed to return.

The reporters were quite friendly and tried to talk to us through the doorway. They were anxiously waiting to see if and when Dr. Gross would call the police to have us evicted. Knowing that if any of us left we would not be able to reenter, some reporters brought us sandwiches and drinks, which we, of course, paid for ourselves. We were becoming disheartened because our ranks had been reduced to eight—five white and three black ministers. I'm happy to report that the three of us Lutherans—Puelle, Neuhaus, and me—stood firm.

I didn't feel as firm inside, though. I had been feeling some personal anguish concerning my involvement in this protest. For five or six years, I had been serving my church and my country as a U.S. Army Reserve chaplain. I had advanced to the rank of captain. I enjoyed representing my church body and serving my God and country in the military and was intent on making the Reserve chaplaincy a career. The problem was that Robert McNamara, the U.S. secretary of defense, had recently made the pronouncement that U.S. military personnel were allowed to participate in civil-rights demonstrations only under certain conditions: if they were not on active duty, if they were not in uniform, and if their participation did not constitute a breach of law and order. This third restriction began to bother me. I finally confided to my fellow Lutheran participants in the demonstration that I felt I was going to have to break ranks and depart from the demonstration. I would not be able to remain with them to the end and be arrested if Dr. Gross did indeed call the police. Then my friend Rev. Neuhaus began to present all kinds of arguments to me concerning why it was so important that I not bow out of the demonstrations. "After all, Sam, white demonstrators outnumber black participants five to three as it is. If you leave, the ratio will be reduced to five white participants to only two blacks involved in the protest. Besides, Dr. Scharlemann is now a general. He will surely come to your aid if you encounter any difficulty with your commission."

Pastor Neuhaus's arguments did not necessarily lead me to continue to participate in the demonstration to the end. Rather, after wrestling with my conscience in fervent prayer, I decided to see things to the end. As far as a possible end to my military career, I placed that in the hands of my Lord and prayed that Secretary McNamara would not see my name in any news reports and come down on me with a vengeance. Thank the Lord he did not! Although the *New York Times* correctly reported that eight clergymen were arrested, it listed only seven names. For some reason my name was omitted. And to think, my name could have lived on in infamy with that account in one of our nation's leading newspapers!

As 4:30 neared, Dr. Gross saw that we were determined to remain in his office. He hated to call the police on a group of ministers, but we wanted him to do so to help make our demonstration successful by garnering media attention. Only after the nine-member school board decided on calling the police did Dr. Gross finally do so.

When the police arrived, they were quite amicable. They were all in plainclothes. They did not order us out or escort us out of the building immediately. One officer in particular seemed to be visibly examining the size of each pastor. After a moment, he asked if we were going to go voluntarily or insist on being carried out. He confided that on the last case where his team had to remove demonstrators, one member of the group weighed well over 300 pounds, and he had insisted on being "carried" out.

The police took us to a jail in Brooklyn, where we were locked up for well over an hour as we waited to be taken to night court. We appeared before a criminal court judge who delivered a homily to us, then set a hearing date for a later time. There we were with common criminals, many of whom were unable to gain release on their own recognizance, as we could. It is not pleasant being locked up and having your freedom taken away, even for an hour or so.

We wondered if we had been successful. Would the publicity help bring pressure on the authorities? Reporters had been on hand as we were led out of the building to the paddy wagon. The television cameras recorded our arrests, and we hoped the story would make the late news because it was already time for the evening news when we were taken into custody. Would the publicity help garner public attention and support in our fight for justice and spur action by the school board to change the conditions of those public schools attended by minority students?

The most visible result of our demonstration and arrest was that shortly after our sit-in Dr. Gross left his post as superintendent of the school system. Whether he voluntarily resigned or was involuntarily relieved of his position, I am not sure. We do know that he was replaced by someone who took positive and remedial action about the deplorable conditions in the New York City public schools.

Another result was that for the first time Hispanic (mostly Puerto Rican) and black citizens had come together to oppose the powers that be. In the old days blacks in the South were expected to refer to all white males, regardless of their age, with the title "Mister." In later years, blacks used the expression "Mister Charlie" as a sarcastic term for the white power structure. Thus it was surprising, encouraging, and humorous at this joint meeting to hear a Puerto Rican leader make a comment to show how important it was for elements of the two minority groups to come together. In part English and part Spanish, he said: "What we need is unity. And if we can continue to work together, we will soon have 'Senor Carlos' on the run!"

Taking Back the Streets

In the mid-1960s, the crime rate in our New York City community was rapidly increasing. Reports of purse snatchings as well as more serious crimes were climbing. The group of pastors with whom I met were wondering out loud as to whether something could be done by the churches. About this time news reports highlighted two incidents that occurred close to our church. One incident involved Alphonse J. Castellana, a druggist, who was killed by two holdup men in his store; another incident involved a mother who was raped by two men in a car at Bushwick Avenue and Weirfield Place, about two blocks from our church. Shortly afterward, a member of my church, Theresa Lickel, called me. It seems she had observed a disabled man walking down the street in front of her house. Three men passed him, heading in the opposite direction. They suddenly turned around and proceeded to attack and rob this man. In addition to reporting this disgusting incident, she asked, "Isn't there anything that can be done about the increasing crime in our community?" Going out on a limb, I replied, "Yes, something needs to be and can be done; furthermore, I will do 'something' myself!"

Not knowing exactly what that "something" was, I later recalled the account of citizens in a Jewish community in Brooklyn who organized themselves into a group known as the Maccabees Safety Patrol of Crown Heights. Their purpose was to suppress the rising rate of crimes being committed in their community. When a rabbi was attacked, it was the last straw. With CB radios mounted in the cars of volunteers, they began to cruise the streets of their community, ready to alert the police at the sight of any criminal activity in their neighborhoods. According to reports, this safety patrol had quite a measure of success. I managed to make contact with one of the former leaders of the group, a young man named Stan Stein. He was most helpful in informing me of how such a volunteer safety patrol operation might be set up.

At this same time, I belonged to a group made up of shepherds of various flocks in the Bushwick section of Brooklyn. Known as the Bushwick Parish, this organization was made up of the ministers of 12 Protestant and Roman Catholic churches in the area. All were determined to remain in the community, sharing ideas and resources and ministering to newcomers of different backgrounds.

When our patrol first began operating, it was big news in New York City and was covered by the local press. Articles appeared in the *New York Times, World-Telegram, Daily News,*. and *Long Island Press.*

Prior to beginning our patrol of the neighborhood, we felt it essential to communicate with the police officials in our community. Because our church was located just inside the border of one police precinct and just over the border of another, we had two different police captains with whom to communicate. Of course we had some parishioners who lived in one precinct and some who lived in the other.

One captain's negative attitude toward the organization of our patrol was based primarily on three objections that he expressed to me when I notified him that our patrol was set to begin. His first objection was that he was sure we would be calling in to report such picayune things as "somebody left the lids off of their garbage cans." I assured him that these were not the kinds of "crimes" we were worried about. Second, he was certain that before long we would begin to arm ourselves with clubs or other weapons. Again, I assured him that we would not; the only "weapons" any volunteer would be allowed to have would be a flashlight. Last he was sure that we would be calling in every time one of his officers took a minute or two off to get a cup of coffee. We again assured the captain that those kinds of issues were neither the purposes nor the concerns for which our patrol was being organized. Eventually, he had to admit that good citizens should be welcome to act as the "eyes and ears" of the police department. Although we never attempted to make a citizen's arrest, we did once convince a young would-be thief to lean against a wall and wait until the police arrived.

Before our patrol was initiated, several people had reported what they felt to be poor service from the police. There were often long waits for police to respond to a call. The longtime residents of the community complained that frequently when reporting a crime, they would receive sarcastic remarks such as, "That's what you get for living in this neighborhood! Why don't you move?" Sometimes officers showed attitudes that reflected not only arrogance but racism toward members of my flock.

It is taken for granted that those who aspire to become police officers come from average American homes and from churchgoing families. However, in many average American homes there still may be found attitudes of prejudice. Therefore, it should not be surprising to find police officers who are influenced by racism. What is surprising, though, is to find law-enforcement authorities who allow such attitudes to be exhibited in the line of duty. I felt it my duty as a Christian pastor to stand against this racism for the welfare of my flock.

10

MILITARY CHAPLAINCY IN VIETNAM

For several years I had been serving not only as pastor of Our Savior Lutheran Church in the Bushwick section of Brooklyn but also as a chaplain in the U.S. Army Reserves. I was the Protestant chaplain for the U.S. Army Reserve 307th General Hospital Unit of New York City, which met for drills at an Army Reserve Center in Queens. The Armed Forces Commission of The Lutheran Church—Missouri Synod extended calls to active-duty status to reserve chaplains of all military branches. It was during the height of the Vietnam War when I received my call. Because such calls are considered divine, I carefully and prayerfully considered mine before accepting it.

It was with mixed emotions and a somewhat heavy heart that I followed the leading of the Lord. It meant leaving the interracial, inner-city congregation in Brooklyn. It also meant leaving the friendship and privilege of working with dedicated and sincere white pastors—Lutheran, Methodist, Baptist, and Presbyterian—all of whom were very much concerned about the physical as well as the spiritual needs of their flocks. These pastors were determined, with their congregants, to remain and minister to the newcomers in the community where God had placed them, rather than relocating to the suburbs. Leaving Brooklyn for active-duty status also meant foregoing opportunities to participate in the civil-rights demonstrations on behalf of my flock.

My first active-duty assignment in 1965 was as one of several post chaplains at Fort George G. Meade in Maryland. This was not too far from Washington, D.C., and I felt it was a good assignment. As long as Protestant chaplains gave priority to conducting a general Protestant service each week, they were permitted to hold a service geared to their specific denomination. At least that was the way it was at Fort Meade at the time. Thus another Lutheran chaplain and I were able to join in conducting a weekly Lutheran Holy Communion service in a chapel that we shared with the Episcopalian chaplain. The Episcopalian service was at 9:30 A.M. and ours was at 11 A.M. We were able to use this chapel for confirmation classes and administering Holy Baptism, as well as for our weekly Lutheran Holy Communion services.

After being stationed at Fort Meade for about a year, I made it known to my supervisor, the post chaplain, that I was ready and willing to go to Vietnam. Soon, I received my orders. My purpose for volunteering to serve in Vietnam was quite clear. My motivation as a military chaplain was the same as when I was a parish pastor: to provide spiritual nourishment through the Word of God and the Sacraments. As a chaplain I was concerned with the physical, emotional, and spiritual well-being of the flock. I was willing to assist the medics in alleviating the physical or mental trauma encountered by our troops, just as in Brooklyn I had fought for justice and against racism. I hoped to model the Good Shepherd, Jesus, showing concern for the physical needs as well as for the spiritual needs of the members of the flock. Ministry to the whole person would be slightly different in war, however, because people would be shooting at me. I trusted that God would protect me against all evil, and if it were His will, that He would bring me safely home again to my loved ones.

On to Vietnam

After making preparations to leave, saying good-byes at Fort Meade, and getting my family settled in Webster Groves, Missouri, I headed to Oakland, California, to await my departure to Vietnam. There an odd thing happened. While enroute to Vietnam, an officer's orders required him to report to the base three days before the departure date. However, he was not required to be housed on the base until the night before the departure date. Thus for the first two nights I stayed with a pastor friend in Oakland; then I went to the Bachelor Officers' Quarters as required. When I was ready to pay my bill for my one-night's stay, the desk clerk said, "Let me see, Captain Hoard, you owe for three nights' lodging." After protesting several times that this was impossible because I had stayed in town with a friend for two nights, the clerk finally discovered that he was confusing me with another Captain Hoard.

Shortly after my arrival in Vietnam, I received a friendly letter from this other Captain Hoard. In his letter, he detailed his family tree, including where his parents were born and the fact they eventually settled in Nebraska and pioneered a family hardware business. He also went into his wife's background, education, and work as a teacher. He apologized that I might have been bored with all the data about his genealogy, but he was wondering if we might be related. I wrote back to him that no, I was not bored at all. I also related some detail about my and my wife's birthplaces and educational backgrounds. Surmising from what he had written that he was Caucasian, I wrote, "It is doubtful that we may be related unless your forefathers once were slaveholders and my people received the name Hoard from them. But I would love to hear from you again." The curious thing was that after he had written me that friendly letter and I had assured him that I would love to hear from him again, I never heard from the other Captain Hoard again. I wonder why.

On Duty

The first thing all troops did upon arriving in Vietnam was to attend a general orientation about the country, along with in-processing personnel information. We learned basic things such as exercising caution in boarding and leaving helicopters, the lay of the land, types of animals, poisonous snakes, the culture, the nature of the enemy, types of booby traps to expect, treatment of prisoners, etc. From the brigade chaplain or the division chaplain we could get general information and supplies, such as small New Testaments for distribution to Protestant troops and rosary beads and crucifixes for Roman Catholic troops. Each chaplain was assigned to a battalion, but other than that, we were on our own.

I was attached to the First Air Cavalry Division. As everyone knows, the cavalry originally moved about by horse, then evolved into a mechanized cavalry with trucks, jeeps, tanks, and amphibious craft. In the Air Cav, foot soldiers are regularly moved about by helicopter. The cavalry is made up of various units: infantry, engineers, artillery, personnel, judge advocate, medical, chaplains, and of course, helicopter and fixed-wing units.

Chaplains who cover infantry units are assigned to serve an entire battalion. We routinely moved about by helicopter to link up with different units and accompany them on their marches or on combat assault missions. I had to provide religious coverage (religious services, counseling, hospital/aid station visitation, memorial services in the field for those killed in action) for troops of a headquarters company and four line companies: Alpha, Bravo, Charlie, and Delta companies. It was quite a spread-out congregation to serve!

My weekly routine was similar to that of a circuit rider. On Friday evenings and Saturdays I tried to be in the trains (or forward supply) area where my bunker was located. There I could do sermon preparation for the coming week, answer correspondence, and counsel with headquarter or line company personnel in the trains area. Sometimes a chaplains' staff meeting would interrupt my tentative schedule of spending time with the line companies. Usually, however, my schedule went something like this: On Sunday I would conduct a service for the headquarters company troops, including clerks, mess-hall crew, and supply staff. After the Sunday service in the trains area, I would jump on the first "Ash, Trash, and Cans" helicopter to link up with one of the line companies. The "Ash, Trash, and Cans" run was the name given to those choppers that carried hot food, cans of water, and resupplies of ammunition for troops in the field. They also transported the mortar tubes and mortar rounds that were too heavy for troops to carry while moving on the ground during daytime missions to search for the enemy. These heavy mortar tubes were used to fire illumination flares all night over villages being kept under surveillance.

After joining the first line company on a Sunday afternoon, I would stay with that company until it was convenient for me to conduct a service. That company might be preparing to depart on a 15-kilometer march to a new position or to go on a combat assault to engage an enemy force. It might be digging in to spend the night. Because of intelligence reports about enemy activity, sometimes it might be one or two days before I could conduct a service. I would set up an altar on whatever I could scrounge, often empty C-ration or ammo boxes or on a rock or ledge.

At first I used real candles alongside the crucifix when I set up for services. But because of helicopters coming in nearby, I had to switch to battery-operated candles with fake glass "flames." I did have a nice silver-plated chalice for Communion services. I usually had a good number of Lutheran men in each of the companies I covered. With men facing death at all times or serious injury from booby traps, those who came to services were eager to receive the Lord's Supper.

What was I to do about our Lutheran close(d) Communion practice when called on to administer the Sacrament of Holy Communion in such a situation? What was right in a situation in which these men were facing death and many were being killed? As a Lutheran Church—Missouri Synod pastor, I uphold our church's policy of close(d) Communion, which is based on Scripture and the Lutheran Confessions. I do not endorse unionism or open Communion. At the same time, as a military chaplain I was guided by LCMS chaplain guidelines that allow for pastoral care and discretion in times of emergency. Warfare certainly qualifies as a time of emergency. But those same guidelines state that no chaplain may be required to violate the religious strictures of his church body. Thus during every service, at the end of the sermon and before beginning the Service of Communion, I made a brief explanation concerning what Lutherans believe, according to the Scriptures, about who is a worthy communicant, about the real presence in the Lord's Supper, and the use of real wine. I laid it on the heart of each individual to determine if he could accept what I as a Lutheran chaplain taught about the Lord's Supper.

Some Roman Catholics going into battle desired to receive the

Sacrament in my services simply because of the shortage of priests. We had three battalions in our brigade and only three chaplains. I was assigned to one battalion, another Protestant chaplain was assigned to a second battalion, and one Roman Catholic chaplain covered the third. This chaplain had to provide Roman Catholic coverage not only for the headquarters company and the four line companies of his battalion but also for everybody else on a catch-as-catch-can basis. Because of this, it was impossible for him to offer Mass regularly for all the troops he had to cover.

In Combat

I have been asked if I had to go on combat operations with the troops. Actually, most of my combat involvement was a matter of circumstances rather than deliberate choice. I often was with one company in the field for two nights and two days before a resupply chopper would be leaving my location to take supplies to a company that was next on my list to hold services. If the company I had joined was going on a march, I was going with them. I had no choice. And I could not get information in advance concerning a company's plans. Just as the troops had their rifles ready for the march, I had my chaplain's kit. But as I prepared to head out, the first thing I would locate was a nice-sized "snake stick" to carry, just in case, while humping through the brush.

I did have a .45 caliber pistol with me at all times so if we were overrun by the enemy, I would be able to defend myself. One time a Roman Catholic chaplain was saying Mass at the edge of a rice paddy in a wooded area, garbed in his vestments. He was shot at by a sniper. When I heard about this incident and learned that the Vietcong also had shot at a medical evacuation chopper, which are unarmed and marked with a large red cross, I opted to abide by the wishes of our battalion commander, who wanted all his chaplains to be armed. What many people do not know is that the Geneva conventions say that chaplains may not be required to bear arms nor may they be prevented from bearing arms. However, if chaplains are captured while bearing arms, their privileges to move about and visit other prisoners may be revoked. Apparently the North Vietnamese or the Vietcong never agreed to adhere to the Geneva conventions. We were encouraged to keep our weapons out of sight because prior to my arrival, the press photographed a chaplain with a .45 caliber pistol on his hip, a rifle in his hand, and bandolier of bullets draped over his chest. The caption read: "Man of God." I carried my gun in a shoulder holster underneath my fatigue jacket. Our Roman Catholic chaplain, Father Phil Lucid, carried his .45 in his chaplain's kit.

Sometimes I would be dropped off to join a company that was preparing to be airlifted to make a combat assault. If I was given this information in advance, it became my decision to join with the company and accompany them on the assault or not. No one ordered me to go nor did anyone try to prevent me. In fact the troops always seemed confident, happy, and encouraged to have me accompany them on a combat mission. And as the military has always known, that's what chaplains are for.

Before lifting troops by helicopter into an area in which enemy forces were believed to be operating, there was a certain modus operandi that the Cav followed. First, the landing zone where the troops would deplane would be "prepped." The prepping involved the big artillery guns. Located several (sometimes twenty or more) kilometers away, these guns would fire rounds on and all around the landing zone for several minutes. During this bombardment, troops to be deposited in that zone would be picked up, flying as usual with the helicopter doors open. Immediately after the last rounds of artillery had been fired, helicopter gunships would zero in on the landing zone and pepper it and the surrounding areas with bursts of rocket fire for about two or three minutes. Immediately after the last rounds were fired, the first wave of choppers with infantry troops would hover over the landing zone, just low enough and long enough for the troops to step on the choppers' skids and jump to the ground. With weapons at the ready, these troopers of the first wave were responsible for charging to the perimeter and securing the landing zone from possible enemy elements in the area so the second wave of troops could be deposited. Even after this prepping, first-wave troopers occasionally would run into a "hot landing zone" and begin receiving enemy fire immediately after being dropped off.

Friendly Fire

One time I was on a combat assault with a company when we found the enemy immediately, or rather, they found us. Just as we were leaving the tree line of a wooded area to cross a rice paddy, enemy forces under cover on the opposite side of the rice paddy opened fire. We scrambled back into the jungle. Although we were hunkered down in a thicket of bushes and trees, the enemy was firing endlessly in our direction. Of course we were returning fire. We could literally hear the bullets whizzing through the leaves overhead. We took a few casualties with men who were careless about keeping their head down and their body close to the ground. After several minutes of exchanging fire with the enemy and with no apparent letup from their side, the company commander had the forward observer radio for helicopter gunships to rain down some firepower from above on the enemy's position. As we waited, our expectation soon turned to shock. Evidently, some pilots had read their maps wrong and our gunships began mistakenly to rain down rockets within the tree line on our side of the rice paddy. Talk about being terrified, shocked, disappointed, angry, and frozen with fear. We were all of these. We were being shot up, momentarily, with "friendly" fire until the forward observer quickly yelled over his radio to the gunships controller: "Cease fire! [Expletive], cease fire!"

One man was mortally wounded on this occasion. He was a sergeant with a little more than twenty years of service time, a father of five who was planning to retire upon his return to the United States. Fragments from the rockets had torn away most of the bottom of his face. All the medic could do for him was to cover his face with a gauze bandage and give him an injection of morphine. As he was growing weaker, I rested his head and shoulders on my chest and began to pray: "O Lord, save Your servant, who puts his trust in You." As I was trying to comfort this man, another sergeant hollered: "Hey, Chaplain, can you help us over here with some of those who were wounded?"

I answered, "I'm trying to help this man right now, Sarge."

Then, unbelievably, he replied, "Yeah, but the ones over here have a better chance of making it."

If the man I was trying to comfort did hear what the thoughtless sergeant said, thank God it was not the last thing he heard. The last thing he heard was me, telling him to trust in Jesus as his Savior: "God loves you, and He forgives you for Jesus' sake. Just trust in Jesus. He suffered, died on the cross, and rose again so we can have forgiveness, and with forgiveness is eternal life. You pray to Jesus. God loves you. Our Father . . ." That good soldier died from friendly fire before we could get him on the medevac chopper that came to pick up our wounded. It was my privilege as a chaplain to be a shepherd to him in his last minutes on this earth.

There were other cases in which troops were killed by friendly fire. A platoon leader, a second lieutenant in one of our companies, was accidentally killed by one of his own men. This young officer had not been in country long. He had attended my services two or three times. The last time he had asked, "Chaplain, why don't we ever sing that hymn 'Stand Up, Stand Up for Jesus'? I love that hymn." I promised the lieutenant that we would sing it during the next service. We did sing it, but he was not there. The night before, he had been checking on the men in his platoon who were on perimeter guard duty. Somehow, as he was moving from post to post, he got outside the perimeter, and as he approached a guard post, he was mistaken for the enemy and shot by one of the men of his own platoon. For this tragedy, I had to provide counseling and encouragement from the Word of God.

The Chaplain's .45

People back home would sometime ask if I ever had to use the .45 pistol I kept with me at all times in case we were overrun by atheistic communists who had no regard for chaplains or religion. I would say no. But that did not mean that I never took my gun out of my holster or never chambered it up. When spending the night with a company on a search mission, I would sleep on an air mattress in my minibunker (a long hole about two to three feet below ground level, with my poncho tied between two trees and draped over the top in case of rain) with my pistol close at hand. That is because inevitably a sniper would sneak over from a nearby village and begin firing at us. Then our troops would begin returning fire. Because I had not been gifted by God to be able to distinguish between the sounds of our bullets and those of the Vietcong, I could never be sure if there were more of them or more of us. Never being certain whether we would or would not be overrun by the enemy, I would first offer up a round of prayers, then chamber up a round in my .45, just in case.

Once we joined battle with uniformed North Vietnamese Regular Army forces. Somehow several companies of North Vietnamese had managed to set up camp near villages not far from our brigade headquarters, where the general ate his meals and attended briefings. Before the battle began, our forces took positions directly in front of the North Vietnamese positions with part of our men deployed on the flanks. Before our ground attack started, we remained in our holes with gas masks on while our choppers dispersed tear gas throughout the jungle where the enemy was entrenched. Next, our big guns fired several rounds of artillery into the area. Their main force began to retreat, but some of their wounded troops remained behind as snipers to slow our advance. We spread out as we moved, following a slowly moving half-track amphibious vehicle that had a machine gun mounted on it, which was blazing away. Two machine gunners on foot were slowly advancing to either side of the half-track. I walked a few paces behind the company commander and his radio telephone operator in case a message came in about casualties from any of the company's four platoons. Suddenly a trooper a few paces to my left screamed as he was shot in the leg by a sniper. Someone yelled that he had seen a muzzle flash in a clump of bushes nearby. We halted so the medic could stop the bleeding and dress the wound. I reasoned that if a sniper was in the bushes, then he could take aim at me next. Therefore, I felt it the better part of wisdom to chamber up a round in my .45. However, thanks be to God, I never had to use my gun for any purpose except target practice.

Sometimes friends would question the propriety of a minister being armed for self-defense and would offer the opinion that Jesus would not have been armed. I would refer them to John 8:59. When certain people were intent on doing Him bodily harm, Jesus made Himself hidden so He could walk right past them. This is something I could not do.

Psalm 91

There were two firefights in which I came close to being killed. I am convinced that it was only because God chose to protect me that I am still here today. As it is written: "A thousand may fall at your side . . . but it will not come near you" (Psalm 91:7). So many others died in Vietnam. It was not that I was unprepared to die. Unlike all other religions, I had a Savior who did everything required by Almighty God to save me from condemnation when I die. In Vietnam I had a strong trust in my Savior, Jesus Christ, the same Savior I proclaimed to others. Yet I did not want to die in Vietnam, so far from home and family.

One time the enemy attacked a company I was with. A couple young soldiers from the company were hit immediately. They fell in the open, a few meters from the edge of a rice paddy. As the rest of our troops were taking cover inside a tree line at the edge of the rice paddy, they were firing in the direction of the enemy. Meanwhile, these two troopers were lying flat on the ground, bleeding, moaning, and frozen with fear.

Fortunately, the enemies' bullets were coming over our heads. The only thing I thought about was trying to help get those troopers back to the comparative safety of the tree line. And if they were fatally wounded, then it was important for me to get to them and assure them of the eternal salvation that Jesus Christ had promised for all those who believe in Him and trust Him.

We had learned how to crawl on our bellies in basic training while live ammunition was being fired over our heads. This was the real thing, and the training paid off. Seemingly by impulse, I began crawling toward the injured soldiers. At about the same time, a medic also left the cover of the tree line and was crawling toward the two wounded troopers. It was a blessing that their wounds—one man was shot in the shoulder, the other in the thigh—did not make them immobile. The medic and I half pushed or half pulled the men to cover. Meanwhile, enemy bullets were steadily flying over our heads as we made our way back to the tree line. If we would have elevated our heads or bodies a few inches as we crawled, we might have been hit. But our goal was to help two frightened, wounded fellow human beings. By God's grace, the enemy fire never came low enough to hit us. Those were two grateful troopers as we helped them aboard the medevac chopper that landed a few meters to the rear of our position. And there was an extra-grateful medic and an extra-grateful chaplain after that hair-raising ordeal. I gave God the thanks and the glory.

Another time I was in the trains area, preparing a homily for the coming week. Someone asked if I was aware that one of our companies had become engaged in a firefight. I had not heard, but I learned that a chopper was preparing to take ammunition to that company, so I hitched a ride. When I jumped off the chopper, I was surprised at the sight that greeted me. While others were unloading the ammo, two young soldiers were wringing their hands in hopeless gestures, crying and trying to console each other. When I asked what was the problem, they began to tell me that their good friend was lying "out there," wounded, and nobody could get to him to help him.

Moved by their emotional distress, I promised them I would get to their friend and help him. After cautiously moving forward through the brush to the company command post, I spied the wounded man. Nobody seemed able to reach him, and strangely enough, all firing had temporarily ceased. I took off before anyone could explain why the guns weren't firing. It was because somebody armed with an AK-47 had a bead on the area surrounding the downed man. In ignorance I figured that if anyone did fire at me, all I had to do was stay as flat and close to the ground as I could and the bullets would pass over my head. I got about halfway to the side of the wounded man when the sniper began firing directly at me. I froze with fear! All I could pray was "Lord, help me!" Hot lead was peppering the ground and coming closer and closer to me. I was bracing and waiting to feel those bullets going through my body. However, the sniper's muzzle flashes gave his position away. Just about every man in our company opened up on his position in a tree. With the sniper silenced, all firing ceased. He had pinned down everyone in our company while the rest of his Vietcong comrades quietly faded away.

When I reached the wounded soldier's side, his pulse was weak. How long he had lain there alone in the open I did not know. He did not respond when I tried to get him to communicate. I began my prayers for the dying: "O Lord, save Your servant, who puts his trust in You. Send him help from Your holy place, and evermore mightily defend him. Let not the enemy approach to harm him, but be unto him a strong tower. Lord have mercy, Christ have mercy . . ."

This was only one of several experiences I had with combat troops facing enemy fire. How was I affected by these experiences? For months afterward, I would have nightmares—reliving the battles over and over, waking up in a cold sweat. I thought of different ways I might have been wounded or how close I had come to being killed. I tried to blot them from my memory by trying not to think of them and by refusing to talk about them. It's the same for a lot of soldiers.

Years later, people asked if I had applied to the government (some even encouraged me to do so) for disability compensation for this disruption in my life. I responded that I was grateful to God that I could carry out my duties as a Christian chaplain, emotional trauma notwithstanding.

A Word from Home

I spent several nights with one company after going on a combat assault with it. I was waiting for the opportunity to conduct a service. On the second night not only did we have to contend with sniper fire but also with a heavy rain that seeped into the crevices in my air mattress. People used to talk a lot about creeping socialism. Nothing can be as bad as cold rainwater creeping down the crevices of one's air mattress in the middle of the night in the jungle in Vietnam. The next morning it was time for the company to rotate to the trains area where it would guard the perimeter around the big artillery guns for a few days. While there, the men could get a shower and some clean fatigues and could possibly hitch a ride to a nearby village for a haircut and some cheap souvenirs.

Before we left the forward position, we had mail call. Imagine the surprise when I found with my mail the November 1967 issue of *Lutheran Forum*, an unofficial pan-Lutheran publication to which I subscribed. Hurriedly scanning the table of contents, I saw an article entitled "The Anguish of the Military Chaplain" written by Rev. Richard J. Neuhaus. He, of course, was a friend and colleague, a former fellow seminarian at St. Louis, and a fellow civil-rights demonstrator in Brooklyn with whom I had been arrested. Sometime after I left Brooklyn, Rev. Neuhaus had become involved with a group known as Clergy Against the War in Vietnam. A saying attributed to him was: "Our military is so determined to help the Vietnamese people that they are willing to do so even if they have to bomb or napalm every one of them." In addition to our personal friendship and bond as cellmates, I knew Rev. Neuhaus (who later left the Lutheran Church to become a Roman Catholic priest) to be a talented and scholarly writer. Thus I was doubly interested to read his article. In it he referred to all military chaplains as "dishonest," "morale officers," and "false-shepherds." He compared chaplains in Vietnam to "a Christian pastor working as a chaplain to executioner-guards at the Nazi death camp at Auschwitz." Rather than becoming angry with my colleague or with what he had written, I found his article somewhat amusing. He had made assumptions about military chaplains simply because their viewpoint on the war differed from his. Among all the chaplains I knew, never had I come across one who suffered from "anguish" about serving in Vietnam.

My response to Neuhaus appeared in the February 1968 *Lutheran Forum* under the title "From the Front Line":

> Picture yourself as a combat military chaplain. You arose before dawn, went on a combat air assault by helicopter with one of your companies in the hope of being able to bring Word and Sacrament to your men whatever time their operations for the day were over. . . . also in case contact was made with the enemy and in a fire fight some of your men might be wounded. You proclaimed the Gospel and celebrated the Eucharist at the edge of a rice paddy, not too far from a known hostile village infiltrated by Viet Cong. After dinner, which was flown out by "chopper," you spent some time counseling with different men. You are bedded down for the night with a poncho "hootch." In the middle of the night you are harassed not only by rain but by enemy sniper fire for close to an hour. Fortunately, again no one is hit. You feel, however, you are making a contribution just by being with the company on their everyday operations before moving on to join another.
>
> With the morning re-supply ship the mail is brought out. You are eager to read one interesting journal, Lutheran Forum. And what do you see after spending a night of anguish dodging the rounds of enemy sniper fire? An article by an old friend and colleague, a fellow pastor, Richard John Neuhaus, on "The Anguish of the Military Chaplain" (Nov., p. 16).
>
> I am concerned that many of my other colleagues may get the impression that I am one of the military chaplains whom he

mentions as speaking of a "deep vocational anguish." One kind of anguish I have in the military chaplaincy comes when I am faced by firepower from the enemy, but it is not the "deep vocational anguish" of which Richard John speaks.

He seems to imply that unless I am constantly leading a discussion with men on battlefield or foxhole, in rice paddies or bunkers, on the pros and cons of the Vietnam War, questioning them on the positions they have already taken, I am a false shepherd. There seems to be a peculiar difference from the way our Lord himself defines a false shepherd.

I am not one of those chaplains whom Richard John describes as contending "that the ministry to individual soldiers can be isolated from the question of what those soldiers are doing." I support what those soldiers are doing as long as they are doing their duty. When they commit murder or atrocities, as in some isolated cases, neither I nor the government supports them; they are tried and dealt with according to military justice.

I am convinced that we are engaged in a just war. I have anguish in seeing men killed, ours and the enemy's. That is why I regularly pray for our men, and our enemies as well, as our Savior taught us. I constantly remind our men that if they have a choice of taking a life or taking a prisoner, to be sure to take a prisoner, and how our Lord would have us treat our enemy—as one redeemed by God.

I certainly want peace just as much and (at times particularly when on the other end of the muzzles of enemy sniper fire) even worse than does friend Richard John. But I can assure you I am not giving aid and comfort and hope to the enemy by my words and actions, in trying to attain that peace.

With his article I disagree most vehemently but I would not think of asking you to cancel my subscription. I found his illog-

ical peace somewhat amusing, interesting and entertaining. I'd
say let's have more . . . if he was not serious.

Samuel L. Hoard
Chaplain (CPT) USA
APO San Francisco, CAL

Personal Contact

In my ministry in Vietnam, I had a rather unique way to become
acquainted with the Lutheran personnel assigned to the companies of my battalion. It soon became general knowledge that
because I happened to be a Lutheran chaplain, I wanted to conduct a personal interview of all Lutheran personnel coming in
country. During the interview, I used my camera and my tape
recorder. I would send the snapshot, identification information,
and a quote or two from or about the man to The Lutheran
Church—Missouri Synod's Armed Forces Commission for possible publication in its monthly newsletter, which was sent to hundreds of service people. I would send the tape-recorded interview
to a colleague and friend, Pastor Walter Loeber, who supported
me and my ministry in Vietnam. At the time Rev. Loeber was
employed by KFUO, a Lutheran-owned radio station in St. Louis
that was located on the campus of Concordia Seminary. (Rev.
Loeber also recorded the organ accompaniment of many hymns
from *The Lutheran Hymnal* so I could use the tape during services
in the jungles or near the rice paddies.)

In the interviews of newly assigned Lutheran personnel, I
would ask three questions. After ascertaining for the audience
who the interviewee was and the congregation from which he
came, I would ask (1) How do you feel about being so far from
home, participating in such an unpopular war? (2) What is the
one thing that bugs you most, that makes duty here difficult? (3)
How do you feel about the demonstrators against the war? Never

did anyone answer the first question by saying, "I wish I had gone to Canada or somewhere to avoid the draft" or "I believe that our country should not be involved in this war." The men were willing to answer their country's call to duty.

The second question brought answers such as "If only I could sleep in a bed on a mattress at night"; "Those bugs, they irritate me at night in the field"; or "If only I could get an ice cold drink of water whenever I want one."

To the third question the men replied: "I believe that the people back home should have the freedom of expressing their opinion and demonstrating but not when their actions and their words are an encouragement to our enemies."

And protest demonstrations were, in fact, an encouragement to the enemy. The following is a tract—written in pitiful English—that included a photo of American war protestors. Hundreds of these tracts were left by the Vietcong in a secluded area through which they knew our troops would be passing. Needless to say, because our troops were not guilty of the conduct described, we laughed at the tracts.

American Servicemen

The Johnson Government had told you that: your coming to South Vietnam is aimed at Helping on request of the South Vietnamese Government to fight Communism. This is nothing but a deceptive contention. U.S. Government with this psychological warfare trick is forcing you into the aggressive war in South Vietnam with an attempt to turn South Vietnam into U.S. military base. The South Vietnamese people are taking up arms against U.S. aggressors and the U.S. set up—trained—equipped—paid—puppet Administration. Fighting against the whole Vietnamese people. They said that: "Americans are dear-friends of the Vietnamese people and give you a card of <Nine

rules> but what about the fact? Everyday, U.S. planes droping tons of bombs into our villages—killing old people and innocent children. In defiance of world sentiment, U.S. troops use poison gas to massacre hundreds of people in Phu yen and other places—toxic chemicals are used to destroy crops, kill domestic animals. U.S. Expeditionary Corps—their Satellite South Korea and the puppet army had carried out the policy <complete kill—complete burn—complete destroy> in their operation. In many places after U.S. aggressors footsteps, no man silhouettes can be seen—No Cock-crows can be heard U.S. aggressors nowadays are more abhored than even Hitler in the past—they hope that with their most barbarous actions they can suppress the fighting will of the Vietnamese people, but they are big mistaken. They can only inflamed the passions of our people. The Vietnamese people have determined to fight until at last they gain independence and freedom for their fatherland.

Armymen! You are sons of the great American people who have freedom and democracy loving tradition, what do you think when you have been forced to besmear the honor of the U.S.A. and commit the most barbarous crimes in the history of mankind. If you are real freedom and justic loving people—friends of the Vietnamese people. Do act: Refuse to obey all orders to carry out mopping up operations to kill the Vietnamese people, to destroy their crops, burn their houses. Demand peace in Vietnam—ask for being sent back to your families—your nativeland.

The South Vietnam Liberation Army

I must confess that one time members of one of the companies in my battalion did put the torch to a Vietnamese home. But this was an exception, not operational procedure. It happened under extreme circumstances. We were sweeping through a vil-

115

lage, searching for the enemy and possible places where a cache of weapons was supposed to be stored. Passing by one home, we saw a group of women and small children gathered in the front yard. The women, entirely ignoring our presence as we slowly marched by, were busily grinding flour. As some of our troopers passed a house a few yards further up the path, a loud explosion sounded as one of our men triggered a booby trap on the edge of the path, blowing away his foot and part of his leg.

Upon learning the fate of their comrade, many of the troopers became angry. They reasoned that the women must have known exactly where that booby trap had been planted because they were keeping their children from playing or wandering into that area. None of the women had bothered to warn us. Therefore, a lesson had to be taught. The house nearest the site of the booby trap would have to go. And it was torched, with the company commander's consent. What bothered me, though, was the belief that the hidden eyes of the Vietcong were watching those women, and us, as we moved through the village on our search-and-destroy mission. If we had been warned of the location of that booby trap, those women would have had to pay a price at the hands of our enemies after we had moved out.

Despite the demonstrations by individuals and groups back home who opposed the war, many people gave concrete support to our troops in combat. I was kept busy with correspondence whenever I spent time in the trains area, writing thank-you notes and acknowledgments for packages from people back home. American Legion posts, Jewish groups, women's groups, church groups, civic and social organizations, and clergy were constantly sending packages in care of the chaplain for distribution. They contained items much appreciated by the troops: lined writing tablets, ballpoint pens, plastic resealable bags in which to keep writing materials and cigarettes dry when wading across streams or caught in sudden rainstorms, presweetened drinks in aluminum-foil packs, cigarettes, hard candy, razor blades, and other toiletries. For me as a chaplain, as it was when I was a pastor, this involved ministry to the physical needs of the flock.

Honoring the Fallen

At one point, the graves registration unit was located within our area of operation. Here, all those who were killed in action were placed in body bags and maintained in refrigerated units until they could begin their sad journey back to their loved ones in the United States. For some reason a directive came down that the body of each individual killed in action had to be seen by a chaplain, who then had to sign an identification card attached to the man's body bag.

Whenever I received a call to come sign a card, I, unlike many chaplains, did not just have those on duty slide a portion of the body bag out of the cooler so I could see the man's face. Rather, I had the workers remove the entire body bag and set it on the ground on its stretcher. Then I followed my own ritual. Although I made it clear to the graves registration personnel that as a Lutheran Christian I did not believe in praying for the dead, I did treat the fallen comrade's mortal remains with respect. I would kneel beside the man's body, begin my brief devotion with the sign of the holy cross, and offer a prayer of thanksgiving that this man, if a member of my battalion, had the opportunity to hear the preaching of the Law and the saving Gospel of Jesus Christ and to receive the Sacrament of the Lord's body and blood. I would offer a petition of gratitude that the man had the honor of serving his country before his demise. I would say a prayer on behalf of his loved ones when they would receive news of his death—that they might be comforted by God's Word. Finally, I would commit the man's mortal remains, using the same words as at a funeral service:

"Earth to earth, ashes to ashes, dust to dust . . . keep these remains unto the day of the resurrection of all flesh." Only then would I sign the man's identification card on his body bag.

I am humbled and gratified to say that the personnel at the graves registration unit confided to me that when they needed to have cards signed and they had a choice of chaplains, they preferred to call me because I treated the bodies with the most respect, which they appreciated.

Three Troubles

During my tour in Vietnam, there were three particular events that I kept recalling and that troubled me for a long time: the Tet offensive, the wound received by fellow chaplain Father Phil Lucid, and the death of Lieutenant Boettcher.

Most people know that Tet was the name of a national religious holiday in Vietnam, a holiday observed throughout the country. It was similar to our New Year's celebration. Because the South Vietnamese troops and people were relaxing and celebrating the Tet holiday, they felt sure that the North Vietnamese troops would likewise suspend all warfare activities. But they were tragically wrong. When the 1968 Tet offensive began, North Vietnamese Regular Army troops, who had infiltrated from the north, joined Vietcong guerillas in the South in an all-out attack on all American installations throughout the country at the same time.

The Tet attack on our battalion was launched after midnight. The day before, the personnel of our trains section—the headquarters company, the medical detachment, a squadron of helicopters, and one infantry company—had begun relocating into what was known as the "I" C area of operation. This area was located as far north as American troops operated. The Marines, who had been based in this area, were scheduled to move out the day after we moved in.

The first thing we did was to dig holes at least six feet long. Then we filled sand bags to place around the holes. This was how we made our individual bunkers, which were finished off with an overhead cover later. The medical platoon had set up a large tent. Several camp cots had been set up for future patients. A few foolhardy troopers, including myself, had opted to try to get a night's sleep there rather than in our partially finished holes, where we should have been. Suddenly, around 2:30 A.M., the medical platoon sergeant poked his head inside the tent and yelled, "Everybody in your holes. We're having a mortar attack." As we rushed out of that tent and dived for our respective holes, many of us were at the same time calling on Almighty God for His divine protection and mercy.

The enemy forces, meanwhile, were stealthily moving closer to our location on foot while we were taking cover from the mortar rounds exploding in our midst. When the mortar attack ceased, some of us complacently returned to the comfort of the camp cots inside the medical platoon's tent. Just as we began to snooze, it happened again. First, one could hear intermittent sounds of automatic weapons. Then came the medical platoon sergeant's booming voice: "Everybody back in your holes! They're starting a ground attack!"

Rushing from the tent, I dived headfirst into my hole. In the darkness, I could not only hear the enemy's shots being fired but also could actually see the muzzle flashes as they approached. Hearing the bullets whizzing overhead and filled with apprehension, I prayed to Almighty God for help. Although I was terrified because of the weakness of my faith, suddenly, led by God in answer to my prayers I am sure, two Marines set up their machine gun right at the edge of my hole. The one began firing as the other steadily fed the long bandolier of bullets. Soon the barrel of that gun was so hot it would have set fire to anything it touched.

My prayers then changed to: "Lord, let them not run out of ammunition." I also recalled the psalm verse I had learned in confirmation class: "Call upon Me in the day of trouble; I will deliver thee, and thou shalt glorify Me" (Psalm 50:15). As fearful as I was, I did call on the Lord God and He did deliver me. The attack was repelled. With no one killed or wounded in our area of operation, we offered prayers of thanksgiving to God.

Later in the war I happened to be at the medical aid station when several wounded men were brought in for treatment, including my friend Phil Lucid, a Roman Catholic chaplain. On that day, two of our companies had become engaged in a firefight with the enemy. I was in the trains area when I received word of the situation. I was getting ready to jump on a resupply chopper and link up with one of the companies. However, the brigade chaplain urged that the better part of wisdom would be for me to go to the aid station rather than the battle. There I would be in a position to minister to the wounded being brought in from both of the companies instead of only one.

When Chaplain Lucid was brought into the aid station, I told him that I had been planning to go out to join one of my companies. He interrupted me: "Sam, don't go out there. It's treacherous! They are in the bushes. They are in the trees. They are everywhere."

As I learned later, Chaplain Lucid was trying to help another soldier carry a wounded trooper on a makeshift stretcher to a safe area when the chaplain was shot in the arm near the elbow. Exactly how serious or life-threatening his wound was I did not know. However, for a priest, his great concern and anxiety was over whether his wound would later prevent him from elevating the host and the chalice in the celebration of the Mass. I could empathize with him because I knew how important this was for him as a priest. It was a ritual that had to be followed when celebrating the Mass. I also could empathize with him because I had been accustomed to celebrating the Eucharist in much the same manner while serving in Brooklyn: the elevation of the host and the chalice; the genuflecting; the use of the Sanctus bells; the use of incense on certain festival days; the use of traditional prayers during the consecration of the elements. The difference, however, was that I followed these practices, rituals, and traditions because of choice and historical precedent, not because I had to.

The death of Lieutenant Boettcher was particularly heartrending. He happened to be one of the Lutheran men in one of the companies I covered. His name struck a bell with me when I first met him because I remembered that one of my roommates at seminary had a book in his library by a theologian named Boettcher, a granduncle of this man. The lieutenant was a handsome, athletic young man, a good leader, and well liked by the men of his platoon. He also was a faithful worshiper at the services I conducted and an exemplary Christian.

One day when I returned to the trains area from a trip to conduct a service for an airborne unit, the men were having chow. As we pulled up in the jeep, Lieutenant Boettcher spotted me and excitedly called out, "Hey, Chaplain, guess what? I was just rotated from platoon leader to a new assignment with headquarters company!" This meant he would no longer have to go on search-and-destroy missions, spend nights in the jungle dodging sniper fire, go on marches during which he might set off a booby trap, or check on his men at their positions on perimeter guard duty at night. He was elated. I was too. This was the Army's policy: After an officer had a few months' experience with companies in actual combat, they pulled him back and allowed him to get experience in other sections, such as headquarters, supply, or intelligence, which would be important if the officer decided to make a career of the military. Incidentally, this was not true for chaplains. We, like the enlisted men, served with the line troops for our entire tour. Even the enlisted men, however, were given assignments in the trains area once they had less than thirty days remaining on their year's tour.

Just moments after exchanging greetings with Lieutenant Boettcher, word came in that his old unit was engaged in a firefight with the enemy. Almost instinctively, the lieutenant felt compelled to join up with his men. This time he was killed. I had wanted to go also, but I was encouraged to report to the aid station to cover the wounded from both companies. Lieutenant Boettcher was not brought to the aid station with the wounded because he was killed in action. It wasn't until later that I learned of his death.

Lieutenant Boettcher's death touched me in a different way than any other individual killed in action, but I don't know why. Perhaps it was because I had just chatted with him about an hour before his death. He was so happy about his new assignment. He had been a good officer who looked out for the welfare of the men of his platoon. He was a good leader, intelligent, and obviously a young man with a brilliant future, whether in the military or in the civilian community. Besides, he was a fellow member of The Lutheran Church—Missouri Synod.

I felt compelled to do something chaplains were not required to do: write to Lieutenant Boettcher's next of kin. Ordinarily this was a responsibility of the company commander. When I decided to write that letter, quite a few days had passed since the lieutenant's death. I had some second thoughts about sending the letter because I did not want to be guilty of setting a precedent, but I wrote it anyway. Then, a few days after mailing it, I began to have second thoughts again. I thought to myself, the man's family has received official word about their loved one's demise. They probably had already held the funeral. My letter might open new wounds, though it was meant to help with the healing and comfort.

I remember saying in the letter that particular comfort might be found in the Holy Communion liturgy, which includes the statement, "Therefore with angels and archangels and with all the company of heaven we laud and magnify Thy glorious name." There we might be reminded of doing something in worship together, along with our loved ones who have gone on before us to be with the Lord.

Whether that letter was appreciated or caused pain troubled me for quite a while after I had mailed it. However, after my return to the United States, I happened to hear from my old friend from Oakland, California, Rev. Herzfeld. It seems he had been addressing a Lutheran Women's Missionary League group at a parish somewhere in California. After his address, a woman who was in the audience asked him if he, by chance, might happen to be acquainted with me. That woman was Lieutenant Boettcher's mother. She said she appreciated my letter a great deal.

War in Vietnam placed men daily, even hourly, in the path of death. In these extreme circumstances—when life itself was in the balance—the eternal truths of God's Word, centered in the precious Gospel of Jesus Christ, were of the greatest interest and concern and brought enlightenment and joy.

11

GERMANY AFTER VIETNAM

In 1968, after my tour of duty in Vietnam, I was assigned to an army post near the town of Crailsheim, Germany. I was delighted because I had traveled in Germany years before, during my days as a seaman. Crailsheim at one time had been a large rail center. During World War II, a German prison had been located there. When German-speaking people would inquire as to where Crailsheim was located, I would proudly respond in my college German: "*Crailsheim ist bei die halbe punkt zwischen Nüremberg und Stuttgart.*" ["Crailsheim is at the halfway point between Nüremberg and Stuttgart."] Crailsheim also is not too far from two other interesting and historic German towns: Neuendettelsau and Rothenburg ob der Tauber.

Rothenburg was a place to which we always liked to direct

tourists. It is one of Germany's oldest walled cities and still has portions of the ancient wall. A celebrated event in the town's history occurred in 1631 when the Protestant town was captured by Catholic troops. The Burgermeister (mayor) of Rothenburg made a wager with the officer in command of the Catholic troops. If the Burgermeister could drink the entire contents of a large tankard of wine (several liters) without stopping, the town could go free. The Burgermeister succeeded and the town was saved, but the good mayor passed out for a whole day. This certainly puts an unusual twist on the whole philosophy of civic duty.

This scene from Rothenburg's history is re-enacted mechanically several times each day. A door to a large window above the entrance to the *Rathaus* (city hall) swings open and a figure of the Burgermeister raises his arm, tilting the tankard in his hand toward his mouth. The Catholic officer, sword in hand, stands beside the Burgermeister.

The town of Neuendettelsau has a special significance for many Lutherans in the United States. In this town in the 19th century there served a pastor whose name was Wilhelm Löhe. He was mission-minded and was instrumental in sending (and securing generous financial support for) pastors from Germany to the United States to preach the good news of Jesus Christ and to establish Lutheran congregations. Many of these congregations were established in Michigan, Ohio, and Indiana. These congregations grew and expanded and in time helped to form The Lutheran Church—Missouri Synod in 1847. Some of the pastors sent to the United States by Rev. Löhe became instrumental in establishing a practical seminary in Fort Wayne, Indiana.

Rev. Löhe was also a pastor who demonstrated his concern for the physical needs of his people in a vivid and concrete way. That was one of several things that I liked about him. Acting in the role of a good shepherd, he established a deaconess program through which women could serve their Lord in various helping ministries. His deaconess program grew and supplied workers in many institutions of mercy. Rev. Löhe also helped found an institution for people who were mentally retarded or psychologically ill, an orphanage, a vocational school, a home for unwed mothers, a hospital for men, and a hospital for women.

On one occasion, I had the privilege of driving Dr. Kenneth Korby, a professor at Valparaiso University at the time, from Crailsheim to Neuendettelsau for a visit. Dr. Korby was one of the outstanding confessional Lutherans in The Lutheran Church—Missouri Synod in the mid- to late-twentieth century, defending the faith against the encroachments of a liberal theology that rejected biblical inerrancy. Like Rev. Löhe, Dr. Korby was a strong advocate of the relevance of the Lutheran Confessions, as contained in the Book of Concord, to the modern church situation. Only this confessional approach to Lutheranism, Dr. Korby insisted, could keep the church from falling into the errors of Protestantism on one side and Catholicism on the other. Interestingly, Dr. Korby—a color-blind Christian if there ever was one—in retirement became pastor of a black Lutheran congregation in Chicago. Thus for me as a black Lutheran pastor, it was especially significant to stand with Dr. Korby on ground hallowed by the sainted Rev. Löhe.

What a thrill it was for me as a Lutheran to worship in Neuendettelsau, giving praise to God with heart and voice with the words of the psalmist of old; hearing the chanting of the pastor with his deep, melodious voice; participating in the responses and finding the location of the antiphon in the hymnbook with the aid of a friendly deaconess who sat next to me; following along with the proclamation of the Scripture lessons as the pastor read; and joining in with the hymns, some having melodies with which I was already familiar. There was no sermon, but what a beautiful worship service at Neuendettelsau!

As a Lutheran pastor, one interesting fact about the city of Crailsheim was that the Roman Catholic church there allied itself with the Lutheran Reformation and subscribed to the Lutheran Confessions. At the time of the Reformation, Martin Luther and the other reformers put down in writing what they confessed to be the truth, based on the Scriptures. These confessional writings also expressed their opposition to the errors of the pope. Based solely on the Scriptures, these writings were published in 1580 in the Book of Concord and have never been changed or revised.

The Book of Concord was endorsed by the signatures of pastors, congregations, mayors, town councils, dukes, counts, professors of theology, and other notables.

It was most fascinating to me when I realized that a Pastor Simon Schneeweis of Crailsheim was one of the original signers of our Lutheran Confessions. I began to feel a connection with an important part of the history of the Lutheran Church. After all, I thought, here I was, walking or driving through the streets of Crailsheim. I shopped in the city and sometimes dined there, not in the same shops or *Gasthausen*, but in the same city in which Rev. Schneeweis lived and proclaimed God's Law and the good news of the everlasting Gospel of Jesus Christ, stressing the cardinal doctrines, I am sure, of the Lutheran Reformation: salvation by grace alone, faith alone, and Scripture alone. So what if I was black? That's my ethnic heritage, and I'm proud of it. But I am Lutheran through and through. That's my spiritual heritage, and I'm equally proud of it. The teachings of the Lutheran Church—that Jesus died on the cross to save us from our sins—are drawn from Scripture alone and are valid for all people of every race. Thus as a Lutheran I felt an immediate bond with this German town. Of course my wife and I, as black people, would love to visit Africa and connect with the history of our forefathers—especially now because archaeologists have been uncovering evidence of the early civilizations there.

Sprechen sie Deutsch?

One source of amusement to most of the Crailsheim merchants was my fearless effort at attempting to use the German language. After all, I had spent four years at Concordia Junior College studying German. I could generally express what I wanted to say in German, but my problem was comprehending everything spoken rapidly back to me in response. Nevertheless, because I was the only officer in the battalion with some ability in German, there were times when my meager abilities were pressed into service.

As post chaplain, I was one of the selected officers of the battalion who regularly met socially with several of the Crailsheim government officials and their wives in an effort to maintain and improve German-U.S. relations. The town officials included the Burgermeister, of course, the police chief, a pastor, a judge, other officials, and some prominent professional or businesspeople. I was always seated for dinner next to the judge's wife because she spoke no English. It was fun and a good opportunity to practice my German. This gracious lady asked simple questions that I could answer, and she politely laughed at all my German jokes. The conversations with her and her husband were always enjoyable. One of my favorite jokes in German went like this: *Es gibt eine Stimme: Karl, Karl, Wo bist du? Die Antwort kommt: Ich bin hier in dem Garten! Ralph, Ralph, Wo bist du? Die Antwort: Ich bin auch hier in dem Garten. Karl, Karl, was machts du? Ich mache nichts. Ralph, Ralph, was machts du? Die Antwort: Ich hilfe Karl!* Of course it loses in translation, but the joke in English is: Karl, Karl, where are you? I'm here in the garden. Ralph, Ralph, where are you? I'm also here in the garden. Karl, Karl, what are you doing? I'm doing nothing. Ralph, Ralph, what are you doing? I'm helping Karl!

Not long after I began conducting Sunday services at the post chapel for the troops and their dependents, I learned about the arrangement my predecessor chaplain had made to secure a substitute preacher when he could not be present. He would use the services of the German pastor of the Lutheran church in town. Only no one referred to a "Lutheran" church. It was always the *Evangelische kirche*. After ascertaining that this "Evangelical church" was not Moravian, Seventh-Day Adventist, or Baptist but indeed Lutheran and that it used Martin Luther's Small Catechism for instruction in Christian doctrine, my wife and I became acquainted with the pastor and his wife. And I continued the practice of using him as a substitute on the rare occasions I had to be away from Crailshcim.

One time the pastor came up with the idea of having a sort of a pulpit exchange. The Sunday before Christmas he preached for me and he invited me to preach in German at his church for one of his Christmas Eve services. What he did not know was that whenever I had previously preached in a German service, I had a former classmate or a colleague who was fluent in German check my manuscript for grammatical errors and errant expressions. Because I didn't have access to such a review, I declined to preach. However, I did take part in his service by reading the Scripture lessons, leading the congregation in the confession of faith with the words of the Apostles' Creed, leading them in the Lord's Prayer, and offering the other prayers.

There was, however, one strange thing about this Christmas Eve service. The Sacrament of Holy Communion was not celebrated. Later, when I inquired of the pastor about why the Sacrament was not celebrated on one of the most sacred festivals of the church year, I was flabbergasted with the pastor's response: "Well, Sam, my friend, some of us just do not believe in the efficacy of Holy Communion." I was shocked at such a remark by a Lutheran pastor! We remained friends, but I no longer needed his services as a substitute for the remainder of my tour of duty in Germany. In the Lutheran Church we believe—at least we are supposed to believe—what the Bible teaches about the Lord's Supper: that Christ is really and truly present in this Sacrament to forgive sins.

There was another occasion when my use of the German tongue was needed. Not long after my arrival at the post, we received a new battalion commander who also doubled as the post commander. This colonel was particularly fair-minded, and he tolerated no ill-treatment or partiality based on race, religion, or background. A young black trooper of our battalion had been granted his request for an "accompanied tour status." When his wife arrived, he made arrangements to rent an apartment in a complex where two white soldiers of the battalion and their wives were renting. When the two white soldiers discovered that the landlord had agreed to rent to a black couple, they threatened the landlord that they would move out.

It so happened that the post commander had the power to declare, for whatever reason he deemed appropriate, any establishment within the German economy off-limits to military personnel. The commander sent a sergeant to explain to the landlord his policy: If you refuse to rent to any Americans because of their race, you will not be able to rent to any Americans at all. When the landlord claimed he could not comprehend what the sergeant was trying to explain to him, I was sent to speak to the landlord, to make clear to him, in German, the commander's policy. My German must have been sufficient because, after conversing with the landlord, the black couple was able to secure quarters from the landlord as had been promised. Of course as a parish pastor I had fought for civil rights in the United States, but it was an interesting turn of events to advocate for racial justice in a foreign country.

There were several occasions during my tour of duty in Germany when I was requested to perform marriages between enlisted men and their German brides. A particular wedding remains in my memory because the enlisted man was 36 years old and his bride was only 16 years of age. Although she had a letter from her parents giving their consent, I had second thoughts about performing that marriage. I inquired of the young girl as to whether her parents spoke English and if she would object if I met them and spoke with them. She said she had no objections, but her parents spoke hardly any English. I assured her that I would be able to communicate with them in German well enough for them to understand, so she made the arrangements for me to meet with her parents.

When I arrived at the home, the young bride's father requested her mother to get out the fine crystal wine glasses. He poured each adult a glass. Then, with great pride, he showed me pictures of his daughter's and his son's confirmation classes. After engaging for a while in "small talk" and polite conversation, the man laid out his philosophy on the subject of marriage. He said if his son was preparing to marry a woman who was much older than he was, he would have a problem with that. But in the case of the man being much older, he had no problem. The only thing that gave him some concern was that the enlisted man might have a wife back in the United States and that he may be taking advantage of his daughter. So, as the saying goes, *alles klappt.* Everything was okay.

One thing stuck with me throughout my ministry as a result of performing weddings during my tour in Germany. Generally, when I performed weddings at the post chapel, the bride's family members and friends who were in attendance rarely understood English well. Thus I adopted the practice of repeating the vows from my German Servicebook. A notable difference from the English version of the marriage rite is in the answer given by the bride and groom when asked if they will love and honor each other and remain faithful until death. The answer in the German is not "I will" or "I do." Instead, the answers are "*Jah, Gott hilfe mir,*" that is, "Yes, God helping me" or "Yes, with God's help." Since my days at Crailsheim, whenever I perform a wedding in English, I ask the bride and groom if it would be agreeable for them to answer the questions with "I do, with the help of God," impressing on them that they do need God's help in living faithful, loving, and forgiving lives with each other.

There was a time when the use of the German language brought me great embarrassment. One morning I was driving from Crailsheim to Stuttgart to attend a monthly chaplains' meeting. I had been warned that there was a small town along the way in which the German police would stop and fine drivers for what we might call DWA: Driving While American. The police ignored German drivers who exceeded the speed limit, but Americans would be stopped and fined. For speeding, German police did not issue tickets but assessed the violator a fine, which was to be paid on the spot. Some of the police officers had money changers attached to their belts.

There I was, dressed in my freshly laundered, neatly creased army fatigues, cruising along comfortably in my American-made Chevrolet, following a German driver in his Mercedes. Then it happened. I saw the flashing blue lights in my rearview mirror. As I began to reduce my speed, the German driver, whom I had been following closely, brazenly began to increase his speed, and he took off in a hurry. I assumed this was the town about which I had been warned. After I had been pulled over, I jumped out of the car and began my "stand up for American rights" protest. "*Ich werde nicht bezahlen! Sie koennen mich vor dem Richter nehmen, aber Ich werde nicht bezahlen! Der Deutscher Fahrer hätte mehr schnell wie Ich gefahren.*" ["I won't pay! You can arrest me, but I won't pay! The German driver was going faster."]

Before I could finish my one-man protest, one of the two police officers tapped me on the breast and said: "Calm down. Calm down. And where did you learn the German?"

"*Ich hab' es in der Schule gelernt,*" I responded, wondering what my punishment would be.

Then the officer said, "We didn't stop you for speeding. We have been trying to catch up with you for several kilometers. We observed you passing on an incline."

I was most ashamed of my needless and unprovoked offensive behavior. The two young police officers were polite, courteous, and conscientiously doing their job. Fortunately, they let me go on my way with only a warning. What a change from the time the racist police officers pulled me over for passing on a hill that night in St. Louis.

Another experience I had in a German town was one that I enjoyed at the time but that later left me shaken and surprised. It also left me with a feeling of gratefulness and relief. The troops had left the barracks and their dependents for field training at a site known as Hohenfels. There they could practice firing weapons. It was in an area where General Patton had been during World War II. The distance was not far, so I had returned to the barracks at Crailsheim to conduct Sunday services for the dependents because the training schedule prevented me from being able to hold services for the troops. After counseling with some dependents and accomplishing some necessary paperwork on Monday, I headed back to join the troops in training at Hohenfels.

When I realized that I would miss the evening meal, I stopped in a small town to shop for a telescope for my young son, who wanted one for playing "pirates." Although it was almost closing time, the shopkeepers graciously allowed me time to search for the item, which no one seemed to stock. I decided that I might as well enjoy a good meal in one of the restaurants in the town. I had *cordon bleu*. The meal, of course, included *Kartoffeln* (potatoes), *Salat*, and a famous German beverage (which I enjoyed, albeit in moderation). While waiting for the meal, some friendly patrons at a neighboring table overheard me speaking to the waiter in German. They engaged me in small talk. After the meal it was dark outside. I ambled down the street a while longer and finally made my way to my faithful Chevrolet. I returned to my quarters at Hohenfels to prepare for training with the troops the next day.

At Hohenfels at that time, officers' quarters were scarce. I was a major by then, but I had to share quarters with a doctor who was a captain of Jewish background. He also happened to be a World War II history buff. When I told him about my pleasant visit, his eyebrows went up. He informed me that that at the end of World War II, the town in which I had stopped had been a Nazi stronghold. When General Patton's troops had surrounded it, the town had refused to surrender and cooperate. General Patton was supposed to have given the town's leaders so many hours to evacuate the women, children, and anyone else who wanted to leave. After the time limit had expired, General Patton leveled the town with artillery fire. The town had been rebuilt, but the bitter and resentful citizens were known to slash the tires of any U.S. vehicle found there after dark. Americans were generally not safe alone in that town after dark.

I was surprised, to say the least. I was shocked at what might have happened to me, but after reflection on what did happen, I was relieved and thankful to God that the hearts of the towns-people obviously had changed toward Americans. Or at least toward one German-speaking black chaplain!

Preaching the Word

One of the highlights of my tour of duty in Germany was an invitation I received to be a summer guest speaker on *The Lutheran Hour,* the Lutheran Laymen's League's internationally broadcast weekly radio program. It was an honor but also a humbling experience. Most of the guest speakers on this program were learned theologians, present or former seminary professors, veterans of the cross who served or had served large congregations, men with doctoral degrees. I did not fit any of these descriptions. I was a parish pastor who had represented his church body by serving with combat troops as a Christian chaplain. I remember being instructed that I would have to mail under separate cover two copies of the tape-recorded sermon to St. Louis to ensure that at least one copy arrived safely for the scheduled broadcast date.

The theme of the sermon was forgiveness. The text, Matthew 18:21–35, was the appointed Gospel for the Sunday on which the sermon was to be broadcast. The response to the sermon was interesting but also somewhat disappointing. Usually when people write in response to a particular *Lutheran Hour* sermon, they mail their correspondence to a specified *Lutheran Hour* program address, not to the speaker. However, I received a couple letters directly from two fellow pastors who happened to be black like me. They both wanted me to know that as a black speaker, I had somehow missed the boat in my message. They felt I had passed up a good opportunity, with an international radio audience, to blast racism in the church and in society. They stated that if another black pastor received such an opportunity, the sermon wouldn't be about forgiveness. In other words, I preached a scriptural sermon on the text I had selected, but as a black pastor, in their eyes, I had missed the boat with my message.

I beg to differ. I think my civil-rights record speaks for itself. And I fought for civil rights as part of my calling as a shepherd of the church. But when called on to proclaim God's Word, my calling is to preach Christ crucified, who takes away the sins of the whole world and is the Savior for all people: Jew and Greek, slave and free, black and white.

I had the opportunity to visit Berlin during the time of the Cold War. The notorious Berlin Wall was still standing. The sight was deeply moving to me as a freedom-loving U.S. soldier. You could see white crosses placed where East German men and women had been shot by Communists as they tried to escape into the free West. The United States isn't perfect; it still has many social problems, racism being the major one. But seeing the Berlin

Wall made me deeply grateful for the liberties enjoyed by all Americans, black as well as white.

This short visit also included a unique preaching engagement. My friend Rev. Ralph Zorn had left his parish in the Southeastern District of The Lutheran Church—Missouri Synod and had accepted a call to the Lutheran Church of Germany in a pastorate in Berlin. When Rev. Zorn learned that I would be visiting Berlin, he invited me to preach at the church where he was scheduled, by his bishop, to conduct services that weekend. This was in a historic chapel that had been built for Frederick the Great in Zehlendorf. Services were conducted there for Americans attached to the U.S. embassy and for others employed or on vacation in Berlin who desired to attend a Lutheran service in the English language. This turned out to be an interesting turnabout. The first (and only) time I had preached for Rev. Zorn in the United States was in the German language at a parish he served in New Milford, New Jersey. Now the first (and only) time he invited me to preach for him in Germany was in the English language.

Unfortunately, I was in Germany for only two years. Most tours of duty last three years. On weekends many of the troops and civilian teachers in the U.S. schools for military dependents had duty-free time in which they could travel. Not so for chaplains. Consequently, I did not have the opportunities that many others had to travel. I regret that I never got to visit some of the historic sites and cities connected with the life and work of Martin Luther, the great reformer who restored to the church the central doctrine of justification by faith. Still I count my tour of duty in Germany as a blessing granted to me by the grace of God. As a Lutheran, it was meaningful for me to be able to experience the homeland of my church.

12

BACK TO CIVILIAN PARISHES

After leaving active-duty status in the military chaplaincy, I accepted a call to St. John Lutheran Church in Kansas City, Missouri. This was the first all-black congregation I had served, and we felt the effects of racism in a rather strange way. The church building was located close to a heavily traveled interstate highway. Frequently, white people, who were traveling through the city on a weekend, would call to ask the time of our Sunday service and would indicate their intention to worship with us. Invariably, someone in the congregation would tell me that just before the service a car with white occupants had driven slowly by our modern, neatly kept, A-frame church edifice. The occupants had stared at the black Lutherans entering the building, then quickly driven away.

While I was serving as pastor of St. John's, we moved to a larger building. We not only had more room for worship and Sunday school but also facilities for a day-care center, a well-baby clinic, counseling, community meetings, and the like. Because the main sanctuary had seating for 200 people and the congregation had a membership of 100, we devised a plan that would bring other Lutherans into the church to share fellowship.

This Kansas City congregation was made up primarily of members who were interrelated in various ways: two brothers who had married two sisters, in-laws, cousins, grandchildren, and so on. Members of several families had grown up as members of Lutheran churches in places such as Mississippi, Louisiana, and Alabama. Some individuals who served as officers of the congregation had preconceived, long-held notions on how Lutheran ministry should be carried out. Although it was not characteristic of all the members, outreach was not high on the list of these individuals, just as many in white congregations do not have this as a priority. Sadly, in later years the congregation was disbanded.

All Lutheran churches in the Kansas City area were invited to take part in the loan-St. John's-a-member plan. For one year, while St. John's was building its membership through invitations to new residents in the neighborhood, other Lutheran churches would send at least one family each Sunday to worship with us. We felt that sharing fellowship in this way would have mutual benefits for the black members of St. John's and for the white members of other churches.

Even in 1971 we should have known that because of the strong influence of racism in U.S. churches, such a plan would not succeed. We did have some response, primarily from congregations of the Lutheran Church in America and the American Lutheran Church. But there was little response from the congregations in the area that were part of The Lutheran Church—Missouri Synod, the church body to which we belonged.

It is sad that many erstwhile Christian people have been deceived by their parents, by official church policies, by teachers, and by secular society. While they hope for the company of heaven, they will not accept fellowship in this world that includes people with skin color and hair texture that is different from theirs. We live in a racist society. Racist beliefs, practices, and attitudes have been allowed to permeate the life of the churches. Racism is a sin against God and against all people, who were created in the image of God. It is a sin of which we must repent.

Thank God we have a Savior in Jesus Christ who forgives this sin along with all others. He came into this world first to the Jews, God's chosen people. The Jews were racially prejudiced. They called Gentiles "dogs." But Jesus Christ was better than His culture. Think of His outreach to the Samaritans and His kindness to the Canaanite woman. He was not prejudiced. Jesus did not reject non-Jews on the basis of race. In His love and compassion He died on the cross and rose again from the dead for all people. He sent Paul, a zealous Jew, to be the apostle to the Gentiles. So now all are included in God's covenant of grace through the forgiveness of sins that is in Christ Jesus. In Christ, God has established the kingdom of God—a kingdom of love in which the enmity between God and mankind has been removed and the hatred of people toward one another is washed away.

While I was serving at St. John's, members and nonmembers frequently complained of the misconduct of some police officers in dealing with minorities. Such charges were often reported in the black weekly press. In this issue I looked not for what I could say in advocacy about the situation but for what I could possibly do. At that time I was a member of the board of directors of the Kansas City area chapter of the Lutheran Human Relations Association of America. Apparently I was the only one on the board who had heard anything about a dedicated black police officer in

Chicago named Renault Robinson. Officer Robinson was the founder of the Chicago African-American Patrolmen's Association.

Having had the privilege of meeting and hearing Officer Robinson as a featured speaker a few years earlier at the Lutheran Human Relations Association of America's Annual Summer Institute, I was well acquainted with the purposes behind the founding of the Chicago African-American Patrolmen's Association and what some of its accomplishments had been. Therefore, I persisted in trying to persuade the Kansas City chapter to invite Officer Robinson to be the featured speaker for its annual banquet. Eventually, the chapter's leaders agreed.

Officer Robinson did his work amid much opposition. Because not all black persons think alike but are individuals with differing viewpoints, opinions, and ideas, some black officers had opposed Robinson's efforts to establish his association. One purpose in founding the organization was to bring about a change in the promotion process, which was not objective and routinely prevented black officers from opportunities to rise in the ranks. Another purpose was to point out the need and elicit the aid of other black officers to see the injustice in and to offer help to curtail the practice of white officers who routinely used unnecessary force when arresting African Americans.

We had high hopes of seeing some wholesome results and changes for black residents who were subjected to police brutality after Officer Robinson made his appearance in Kansas City. We had advertised and promoted widely his scheduled appearance, or so we thought. We advertised in the daily press and the black weekly press. We made public announcements. We invited black police officers, pastors, and members of various church denominations, as well as members of organizations such as the NAACP and the Urban League.

However, we had dismal attendance for the event. It was somewhat understandable why some of the black Kansas City police officers were reluctant to be seen with a police officer tabbed as a "radical" in some law-enforcement circles. Fearful for the security of their careers, many did not have the gumption that Officer Robinson had exhibited. He became unpopular. When unjustly threatened with being fired, he countered with the threat of a suit against the police department and had legal backup ready to assist him. When he was given undesirable work assignments—the midnight shift for patrol duty or directing traffic in the Loop in Chicago on the hottest or stormiest days—he performed his duty without complaint. Robinson had to be extremely careful not to be late for duty and never to violate the slightest code or rule; however, he successfully persevered and accomplished his goals.

We had hoped that having Officer Robinson speak would be helpful in bringing about solutions to similar problems about which African Americans in Kansas City were complaining. Although we know that in Bible times shepherds carried a rod or staff to protect the members of the flock from marauding thieves or wolves or lions, we know that shepherds were not always successful. In our case, maybe some seeds were sown that much later had positive results after Officer Robinson's visit, with some healing of the problems between members of our flocks and some Kansas City police officers. I don't know. But it was my duty to act in the role of advocate on behalf of members of my flock as well as others.

Ministry in Orlando

In 1972 I received the call to Our Savior Lutheran Church in Orlando, Florida. After prayerful consideration, and after consulting with the officers of the Kansas City congregation and with the officers and some members of the Orlando congregation, I accepted the call. Although now retired, I have been in Orlando since 1972.

Our Savior was built as a unique departure from the general rule on establishing mission congregations in the Florida-Georgia District of The Lutheran Church—Missouri Synod. The church edifice was built in the mid-1950s before a congregation had been formed. It was on a main thoroughfare at the edge of an area where a large number of modest-income single-family homes were being built with black families as the target market. The congregation was integrated but predominantly black. It was located not far from Disney World. Here, too, we received many calls from white vacationers looking for a church to visit only to see them enter the parking lot, look at the black members, and drive away. The white Lutheran visitors in Florida weren't any more sanctified with respect to race than those in Missouri.

In meeting with representatives of the Orlando congregation before accepting the call, I learned that Our Savior was one of several Lutheran congregations that followed the practice of celebrating the Eucharist only once a month. However, I was used to celebrating the Lord's Supper on a weekly basis. This is the best practice of the church on earth, and Lutheran congregations at their best follow suit. After explaining the scriptural precedent and the Lutheran understanding of the working of the Holy Spirit through the means of grace, we agreed on a gradual move from once a month to twice a month and eventually to weekly Communion services. This, of course, made a tremendous difference in the spiritual growth of the members. How could it not?

Sometimes we would hear a disgruntled former Lutheran complain that the liturgical service was boring, dry, unemotional, and routine. In fact, this liturgical consistency worked as an advantage for children and those adults who happened to be illiterate. In learning the different parts of the liturgy by repetition, they could participate in worship as well as their neighbors who could read from the hymnal. The service we employed at Our Savior was anything but dry and boring. Besides the changing of the altar paraments to different colors according to the seasons or Sundays of the church year, I used the chasuble, which gave added color to the chancel and altar area. I also would chant the appropriate parts of the responses or collects. On two or three Sundays of the month, I would chant the lessons. Eventually, the elder who was scheduled to read the Old Testament reading, once he learned, also chanted that lesson on the Sundays when the other lessons were chanted.

We followed the tradition of administering the Eucharist as was done in Luther's day—according to the Lutheran Confessions. Thus it was done with solemnity and dignity. I was accustomed to genuflecting; I used the Sanctus bells during the consecration of the elements; and I used incense on certain feast days. This had been my practice when I served St. John the Evangelist Lutheran Church in Brooklyn.

It is interesting to note how I happened to acquire the censer and Sanctus bells that I used in services at Our Savior. At one point not long after my ministry began at Our Savior, the local pastoral conference agreed to sponsor a Mass, or Holy Communion service, in a manner similar to the way one would have been conducted in Martin Luther's day. I remember that many of the participants in the service were retired pastors, some of whom were former presidents of districts in The Lutheran Church—Missouri Synod. I remember that Rev. Kurt Biel served as a crucifer, and I was asked to chant the Gospel for the service. When that memorable service ended, someone asked what was going to be done with the censer and the Sanctus bells. The answer came to give them to me because I would use them. Thus I acquired the items that I had been accustomed to using in Brooklyn. I used them at Our Savior in Orlando until the day I retired.

When I assumed the pastorate at Our Savior, the organ was located in the rear of the church, which is where the choir was located as well. Usually, one would find the organ and the choir in the balcony in the rear of Lutheran churches, but Our Savior had no balcony. From time to time a member of the choir or a new member of the congregation would inquire why our choir sang from the rear of the church rather than the front like other Protestant churches so people could see them. Repeatedly I would explain that the role of the choir in Lutheran churches was to augment the worship and singing of the congregation, not to entertain.

No one can truthfully say that the Lutheran liturgical service is dry, dead, or unexciting. On some Sundays the entire service was chanted by the pastor and the appointed lessons for the day chanted by the lay reader. The Sanctus bells were used when the Sanctus was sung during the consecration of the sacramental elements and as the pastor elevated the bread and the chalice at the altar. Besides using two acolytes as torchbearers and one to hold the lectionary from which the Gospel was either read or chanted from the center aisle amid the congregation, an acolyte was also used as a crucifer to lead the entrance and departure of the clergy at the beginning and ending of the service. On days when incense was used, a thurifer would be included in the processional and recessional of the clergy, crucifer, and torchbearers.

On major festival days of the church-year calendar, the sweet, pleasant, and churchly smell of frankincense would permeate the church as the Communion vessels (which were covered), the lectionary, and the altar itself were censed. At funerals, when the Sacrament was celebrated, the coffin of the beloved deceased member would be censed before the benediction.

Some who are not up on their church history have made spurious charges that following the Lutheran liturgy in worship is using something from the German culture. What they do not realize is that liturgical worship transcends yet includes all cultures. The liturgy has been used for centuries in Egypt, Africa, France, England, the Ancient Near East, Russia, Italy, and Greece, to name a few places other than Germany. Liturgical worship is truly multicultural.

As a response to some of my fellow African American Lutheran pastors who are convinced that black people cannot be gained as members for the Lutheran Church when liturgical worship is used, I will quote a letter of mine that was published in the July 2000 *Reporter*, an official publication of The Lutheran Church—Missouri Synod.

> Fellow Lutherans should be aware that not all African-American Lutheran pastors (or lay persons) agree with certain pastors in our Synod who believe that the American culture must somehow affect African-Americans in a very strange way when it comes to adjusting to religious practices in the United States.
>
> When African-Americans become educators, lawyers, doctors or enter other occupations, they have no problem adjusting to the customs, language or social practices followed in those occupations. Yet our Synod sanctions and supports a group of African-American pastors who promulgate the claim that most African-Americans are not intelligent enough to comprehend, appreciate or relate to a liturgy that goes back to the 5th century Coptic church in Africa. . . . Part of the problem may be confusion of emotionalism and ignorance with Black culture. Emotional outbursts, such as shouting and jumping, were taught and learned to be improper in schools and libraries, at concerts or lectures, or in court sessions. Such behavior is attributed to poor manners and ignorance. Unfortunately, ignorance became a part of the African-American culture by

design when slave owners disapproved of educating slaves and when unscrupulous politicians made unjust laws to try to prevent African-Americans from becoming educated. But that was long ago.

Today, if people refuse to control their emotional outbursts in church, where others have come to worship, should such people be encouraged in their disruptive and ill-mannered behavior? Can such behavior be justly attributed to the Spirit of God, who desires things to be done decently and in order? Or should ignorance (not knowing any better) be discouraged? I believe it should.

Is a so-called Black Hymnal really necessary for intelligent African-Americans to relate to scripturally-centered worship, to appreciate the liturgy of the holy catholic church handed down through the ages, even from Ethiopian Christians? I believe not.

Shortly after slavery, when it had been illegal for African-Americans to learn to read and write, it was necessary for pastors and other worship leaders to "line the hymns." The leader speaks the line of a hymn stanza, then the people sing it. It was also necessary to sing hymns with simple verses with the same lyrics repeated over and over. But is it necessary or responsible to perpetuate and reinforce this part of African-American culture today? Again, I believe not. . . .

A final question: What will it take to prod our Synod to begin to help fellow Christians—fellow members of the Synod especially—of different cultural, racial and ethnic backgrounds to build bridges of understanding, of acceptance and love? The goal would be not only to *build* those bridges, but, through Word and Sacrament, to enlist the Holy Spirit's aid in motivating our people to cross these bridges instead of perpetuating and encouraging devices that help reinforce stereotypes and strengthen artificial barriers between fellow believers.

To feed the flock spiritually, I based my preaching on the appointed lessons of the liturgical church-year calendar, always focusing on Law and Gospel. I taught the flock about sin and grace. I taught the members about sanctification, that is, holy living by aid of the means of grace (God's Word and Sacraments) through which God the Holy Spirit operates in people's lives. I taught people about God's great love and forgiveness, of which people are in constant need.

Besides regular Sunday morning adult Bible classes and Sunday school classes for children, we held midweek Advent services prior to Christmas and midweek Lenten services prior to Easter. To give the Sunday school Easter-egg hunt a spiritual focus, we used what we called the "alleluia egg," which was a goose egg and larger than the dyed chicken eggs. Before the hunt began, the story of the Passover was told to all participants. During the hunt, the child who found the "alleluia egg" and could retell the story of the Passover would win a special prize—a pound cake made in the shape of a paschal lamb.

At one point we employed a system of reading the Bible in one year. A faithful few participated in these midweek Bible-reading sessions. Also for a period of time we held midweek prayer services, encouraging members to pray with one another, aloud, for their own needs and for the needs of others.

Teaching and using the *Evangelism Explosion* methodology of witnessing was another effort to help feed the Word of God to those members of the flock who participated and to get members involved in outreach for God's kingdom. This method involved diagnosing an individual's spiritual status on the basis of answers to these questions: "If God should call you from this life on this very day, are you sure that you would go to heaven?" And "If you should be brought to the very gates of heaven and God would ask you, 'Why should I let you enter into heaven?' what would you say to Him?" Participants in this evangelism method were prepared to witness to the certainty of heaven for true believers and to the fact that heaven is not earned by what people themselves do but by what Christ has already done for all mankind. After answering any further questions that may have been raised, members were prepared to invite people, if they had no church home, to worship with us and to learn more of what the Bible says about Christian living and the way of salvation.

There were other ways in which I tried to be a good shepherd and show concern for the spiritual needs of the members of the flock. Besides regular visits to hospitalized members, I regularly took the Sacrament of Holy Communion to shut-in members. As far as dealing with members who had become inactive, we were more concerned with giving them more time and repeated visits to try to reclaim them as active members at our church or some other church than rushing to excommunication. Overall, our members were content to worship in the traditional Lutheran way. And in all these things, I was an ordinary Lutheran pastor like my white brothers (and Hispanic and Asian and European and Middle Eastern and East Indian and African and Slavic and Russian)—happy to minister to God's people with the Good News of salvation through Jesus Christ alone.

Caring for the Flock

In showing concern for the physical and mental well-being of members of the flock, frequently I would find it helpful to get results by turning to the public forum in writing. One time certain young people (members of another flock) appealed to me for help with a school problem because of my involvement with social issues in the community. I responded to their plea, after other attempts at amending the situation had failed, with the following letter to *The Sentinel Star*:

Black Face Skit Offends Black Youths

Winter Park High School still is living with the vestiges of the Old South. It used to be that blacks, Catholics and Jews were the major victims of ridicule, scorn and unfair treatment by the racists. But today at Winter Park it is just the blacks.

Recently a teacher let a white pupil under her supervision go on stage in an assembly in black-face and use dialect in a demeaning and insulting imitation of a black person. Although several black students complained, the principal evidently thought this was clean, innocent fun and permitted it to be repeated in a second assembly.

This, incidentally, is surprising because he's the same principal lauded by your editorial for taking the "right kind of action" when he called the police and 20 students were arrested for smoking marijuana.

Many people wonder why blacks in integrated schools frequently segregate themselves in small groups. When their superiors or leaders permit such affronts as this, it is no wonder blacks seek support and security from mutual companionship.

Whether as a result of my protest I don't know, but that principal was, not long afterward, quietly moved to a different position. There were no further incidents of this type, and the young people of my congregation were greatly encouraged.

I used to wonder why blacks in an integrated school or other integrated setting would voluntarily segregate themselves when they did not have to be. Then I began to learn why: Some blacks need support when they are rebuffed, scorned, or somehow mistreated by someone who feels superior because of race. This has never been a problem for me. When I offer a smile or a friendly greeting to another human being and the individual looks directly at me and gives no response—or even looks at me with disdain— I don't need support. I sigh a prayer. Perhaps the person received some tragic news about a family member or loved one. Maybe the person needs a prayer of mercy because he or she has become a victim of someone—a family member, a friend, a teacher—who has taught the person to hate, to feel superior to other human beings because of race. People do not become racist, they have to be taught. So I ask God to help the ones (if they should still be living) who mis-taught this individual, and I happily go on my way.

The Riots

One may cite numerous cases wherein members of the flock have been abused at the hands of bad law-enforcement officers who serve alongside their community's finest. While serving with the National Guard, I was personally involved in one case in which a man was brutally shot and killed on a street corner.

In 1980 a jury in Tampa, Florida, handed down a verdict acquitting four white police officers who had been accused of the beating death of a black insurance man, Arthur McDuffie. This set off what was probably the most deadly race riot in the history of Miami. Florida Governor Bob Graham ordered more than 3,000 National Guard troops to Miami to assist the hundreds of police officers and state troopers who were patrolling the streets.

Governor Graham's orders came on a Sunday afternoon while the battalion to which I was assigned was holding its monthly weekend drill. When the troops of headquarters company departed from Orlando in a convoy headed for Miami, my chaplain's assistant and I were part of the convoy. Additional convoys of National Guardsmen also were deploying, including other companies in our battalion, which were leaving from armories in Sanford, Eustis, Leesburg, Dade City, Clearwater, and Lake Wales.

As our convoy approached Miami in the early evening, we could see smoke and some flames in the distance. It looked as if the city had been bombarded with artillery fire. It was disheartening, to say the least, to realize that this was an American city. What was also disheartening to me was that this riot was precipitated by injustice—the involvement of the four white police officers in the death of the black insurance man and the Tampa jury's acquittal.

In our first few days of duty in the city, our guardsmen assisted Miami police officers and Florida state troopers in blocking or rerouting traffic at certain street corners and by patrolling near businesses and residential areas. It was surprising to hear the attitudes of some of the police officers the guardsmen were assisting. The officers were unfriendly, unresponsive, and arrogant toward the people whose safety and property they were sworn to protect. Some guardsmen noted that when some of the residents offered police officers a cold drink or a stool to sit on, most officers would not only refuse to acknowledge the offers but would look at these residents with contempt.

Early each morning, just before the troops assigned the duty of assisting police for the day were dismissed from their formation, I, as the battalion chaplain, was given an opportunity to say a word and offer a prayer for their safety and God's protection. And we needed God's protection. One morning as a group of guardsmen were about to exit from the rear of their truck, someone hurled a Molotov cocktail into the truck. Almost instinctively, someone caught the bottle and tossed it over the side, where it harmlessly exploded into flames.

Later that same day, I began to make my rounds, visiting some of the soldiers of my battalion at their posts, checking on morale, asking about any problems back home, etc. As my jeep driver pulled up to one corner to let me out, I saw a man who had been shot by the police lying on the ground and moaning in pain. At the time I did not know why he had been shot. He looked as if he had been critically wounded. The paramedics had just arrived and were trying desperately to locate a vein to inject morphine. He needed help—not only physical help but also spiritual help.

While invoking the presence of the triune God as I made the sign of the holy cross, I took the man's hand and began to pray close to his ear, as I had done for so many wounded men in Vietnam: "Lord have mercy. Christ, have mercy. Lord, have mercy." Then I began to encourage the man to talk to Jesus in prayer. I kept assuring him that God is a loving, merciful, forgiving God, which is why He had His Son, Jesus, die for our sins and rise again from the dead. I assured the man that if he could hear me and he was sorry for his sins, God would forgive all his sins. I told this man to trust in Jesus. If he could hear me, I whispered, he should pray the Lord's Prayer in his mind with me. "Our Father . . . Lord, have mercy. Christ, have mercy. Lord, have mercy." Suddenly, as I knelt beside him and prayed, he began to breathe loudly and swiftly and his body shook uncontrollably. Then he died.

Assisting the Miami police officers at the site of the shooting were two guardsmen from one of our companies. One of these eyewitnesses was black and one was white. In an effort to get an unbiased report of what might have happened to cause the police to shoot and kill this black man, I asked each guardsman, independent of the other, to relate to me his version of what had occurred to cause the shooting. Each guardsman's description of the events leading to the shooting was essentially the same. Although descriptions of the events appearing in the press differed, these guardsmen were not biased toward or against the police, nor toward or against the man who was killed.

According to the guardsmen's accounts, there were some extra sawhorse barricades near the ones which were being used to block the entrance to the street. This man, who happened to be black, began to ride a bike between these barricades and the ones block-

© The Miami Herald/David Walters

ing the street. A white Miami police officer ordered the man to cease riding his bike among the barricades. This man ignored the warning. To add insult to his defiance of the police officer's order, as he pedaled his bike, the man displayed a knife and pretended to shave. As he continued to ignore the police officer's order, he even went so far as to wave his knife tauntingly in the direction of the police officer. He was not near enough to be a threat to the police officer's safety, but the officer shot the man with his service revolver. News reports identified the man as Allen Mills.

Mr. Mills was in the wrong, no question. He should have obeyed the officer's command. But he posed no threat and did not deserve to die. Police have procedures to handle these situations. He could have been peaceably restrained and taken into custody. The only possible conclusion is that the police officer took the opportunity to shoot a black man because of racist hatred—and this in a city already torn apart by racial violence. This bad cop is an example of the few who are a disgrace to the many fine and dedicated officers found in law-enforcement careers throughout the United States. I'm glad I was able to minister to Allen Mills in the final moments of his life. May God have mercy on his soul and on the soul of the police officer who killed him.

When some of the comparatively few rotten apples in law enforcement cause harm to people, pastors must speak out and take action as advocates in defense of the victims. There are God-fearing officers, along with others sincerely dedicated to the honorable principles of their profession. Sometimes these individuals observe fellow officers who unlawfully act as judge, jury, and avenger toward suspects. When this happens, the dedicated officers need to speak out for justice.

There are legal organizations and national citizens' associations that practice advocacy full-time. They solicit membership fees to support their cause. But love is a great antidote for injustice. Pastors who live by God's Word ought to be advocates for members of the flock and others harmed by injustice.

Does it seem out of place for a pastor who strives to be a good shepherd to denounce such injustice, even when it is found in only a few misguided law-enforcement officials? Of course when I use the word *justice*, I am not speaking in the theological sense. I am talking about the principle of moral rightness, conformity to moral rightness in action or attitude, fair treatment. In other words, treatment of one's fellow human being as one would expect when one loves other people as God commands and desires.

A good shepherd regularly proclaims God's love for others, a love God demonstrated by sacrificing His Son on the cross to pay the price for the sins of all mankind and raising Him to life again. It is consistent for such a shepherd to work for justice in practical ways. As Scripture teaches: "Seek justice, encourage the oppressed. Defend the cause of the fatherless, plead the case of the widow" (Isaiah 1:17). "Let justice roll on like a river, righteousness like an never-failing stream" (Amos 5:24).

CONCLUSION

My purpose is twofold in relating some of my experiences from 35 years in active parish ministry and as an Army Reserve chaplain, plus the eleven years spent after high school in preparing for the day of ordination as a Lutheran pastor. One is to encourage young people of all races not to throw in the towel during their efforts to accomplish their goals. A second purpose is to give younger pastors pause for reflection on how being a good shepherd involves concern and effort on behalf of the physical as well as the spiritual needs of their flocks.

When Dr. Martin Luther King Jr. was launching nonviolent resistance, organizing sit-ins, and voluntarily going to jail in protest of the unfair treatment that African Americans experienced because of government-sponsored and government-enforced segregation laws, voices of criticism were heard from both the black and white communities. Some critics, of course, were sincere and well-meaning. Others simply favored the status quo. Criticisms included "You can't fight city hall!" "You're fighting a losing battle!" "You must go slowly in working for changes when it comes to race relations." "You cannot expect change for betterment in conditions until you first change people's hearts."

The truth is that God alone can change people's hearts. Going slowly in seeking relief and curtailment from unfair treatment is well and good for those who are not on the suffering end of the effects of that treatment. Prophets in the Old Testament challenged the status quo, taking their protest to the highest levels of government, with Moses a prime example. If Moses had given heed to his critics, would the children of Israel have been released from bondage?

In the New Testament the apostles were arrested and threatened with jail by the civil authorities because they were preaching about the love of God in Christ Jesus for all people. But what did they do? They went right back out and continued to preach about God's love for all mankind. They willingly went to jail for their opposition to the ban on such proclamation given by civil authorities. While Scripture admonishes that we are to give to Caesar the things owed to him (Luke 20:25), it also admonishes "We must obey God rather than men!" (Acts 5:29).

While some of my fellow pastors may see the good shepherd's role as being concerned only with the spiritual nourishment of the flock, I do not fault them for their conceptions of what being a good shepherd means. However, when one has lived under some of the consequences of racist actions, such as degradation, humiliation, inconvenience, unfair treatment that leads to pain and suffering, as I and other African Americans have experienced, then one might take a different perspective concerning the role of a good shepherd. That role is confronting government officials as leaders and advocates for the physical needs and welfare of their flocks. After all, the concern for fair treatment of members of their flocks will be with us for many days in the future because of mankind's sinful nature. For what is fair treatment for the welfare of the flock if it is not included in the *love* God wants people to have for their neighbor? It is part of the love God desires all people to have for one another in this world.

For all those who have by faith accepted the redemption of Jesus Christ as their own, dare we shirk our responsibility to help spread this love, of which fair treatment of our neighbors is an essential part? As Martin Luther makes so clear in the Small Catechism, this is the ethics of the Fifth Commandment: "We should fear and love God so that we do not hurt or harm our neighbor in his body, but help and support him in every physical need."